COME AND FOLLOW ME

"... Master, all these things I have ob-served from my youth.

And Jesus looking on him, loved him, and said to him: One thing is wanting unto thee: go... and come, follow Me.".

Mk. 10: 20-21

Come and Follow Me is a book prepared for publication by the Franciscans of the Immaculate [marymediatrix.com], POB 3003, New Bedford, MA, 02741-3003- Translator: Fr. Alphonsus Mary Sutton, FI

© 2000 Franciscans of the Immaculate
All rights reserved
ISBN: 1-60114-010-X

Imprimatur   ✠ Most. Rev. Sean Patrick O'Malley
OFM Cap., Bishop of Fall River
Massachusetts, USA
January 1, 2000
Solemnity of the Mother of God

Come and Follow Me

Fr. Stefano M. Manelli

Preface

"Come follow Me" (Mk. 10:21)

" Behold, I come, O Lord!" (Heb. 10:7)

The life of man is framed by these two statements, the first from God, the second from man, request and reply.

Where the request find no reply, what kind of life does such a man lead?

A failed, a tragic life.

The gospel recounts in this regard the failure of the rich young man to reply to the call of Jesus and concludes with his "sad" departure from Jesus (Mat. 19:22).

Jesus is love, is joy, is life. When He chooses "His own", it is to give them exclusively all His love, His joy, His life. Who does not answer, who does not accept, like the rich young man condemns himself to the "sadness" of life.

Perhaps this is the point where a fruitful meditation might begin: does not the fact of so much "sadness" in the lives of men— not withstanding the deceptive appearance of their artificial paradises— stem ultimately from the failure of so many to respond to the calls of the Lord? It surely seems so.

Another reflection. Virginal love, consecration to God, religious life are the sources of peace, of joy, of virtue in man and between men. The rich young man who did not accept the call of Jesus left "sad" and brought his "sadness" among men. Who responds, instead, and "follow Jesus" is filled with joy and carries that joy within himself and shares that joy with others. Recall St. Francis, St. Philip Neri, St. Thérèse... For this the Church exults in her "elect", in her consecrated, and her exultation fills the whole earth.

Young boys and girls who read this, to you are offered these pages for the sake of your "vocation", your destiny. For no mere diversion did the Lord make this little book fall into your hands. It can lead you to find the "hidden treasure" buried in the unexplored field of your heart: the "hidden treasure" of your vocation. If you are to find it, do not delay, do not waste time, but hasten to "sell all" to possess that treasure (Mt. 13:44) and then what riches and joy will over flow from your heart and from your life, making the entire Church in heaven and on earth rejoice!

May our Lady be the star guiding you in the footsteps of Jesus.

Table of Contents

WHAT IS A VOCATION?

What is your vocation?

Young people every now then will hear this question put to them in one form or another. Almost every time it seems to catch them by surprise and they feel some embarrassment about answering. They quickly realize that it is a serious question, but usually, they do not know what to answer, and they try to dodge the issue by an evasive "Who knows?.. I will think it over ... I will see later on."

They may never have seriously reflected on the word "vocation", and on hearing the term put to them this way unexpectedly, the sound of it seems almost strange and mysterious.

What does *vocation* mean?

It comes from the Latin *"vocare"*, meaning to *"call"*... Thus we say that every vocation is a *call* addressed to man.

From whom does this call come?

It comes from God, who is the Master of man's life and man's death.

It is God who gives us being and causes us to continue to be, so that *"in Him we live and move and have our being"* (Acts 17:28).

What does God call us to?

God calls, first, every person into human existence. Then, He calls him to carry out some mission in his life whereby he is to grow in holiness and in this way to earn Paradise.

St. Ignatius of Loyola beautifully set forth the doctrine: "Man was created to give praise, homage and service to God, Our Lord, and in this way to save his soul. Other things that are on the face of the earth were created for man to help him achieve the end for which he was created."

This call to human existence and to holiness is the vocation of all — of every man that is born into this world.

But the "call" to gain holiness by fulfilling one's God-given mission during the course of his earthly sojourn determines the *right state of life* for each individual to adopt. Thus, one who perceives that he is called to matrimony, has the vocation to marry and must live in the state of matrimony. One who perceives he is called to the priesthood must carry out his vocation in the priestly state. Someone finding himself called to the consecrated life, must respond by embracing the religious state. One who finds he is called to missionary life, must make his life that of a missionary .

One can also consider "vocation", in its broadest sense, as a call to one of the professions or other human careers, especially the career of those who, without consecrating themselves to God, remain unmarried, completely and exclusively dedicating themselves to the occupation of physician, teacher, artist, farmer, mechanic, etc.

Each boy and girl has his own particular "vocation" to fulfill in life, the vocation assigned to him as his way to reach the Kingdom of Heaven. Everybody has a call from God to which he is expected to respond, so as to faithfully fulfill it in order to attain salvation.

The task of determining what is one's true vocation is certainly not something one does with effortless ease. But one must do it, because it is something bearing on everyone's temporal and eternal destiny.

With a fatherly wisdom Pope John Paul II warns us, "Everybody, especially if he is young, must intelligently ask himself the fundamental question about Christian life: *'What is it that God calls me to?'"*

There are perhaps many who do not ask themselves this "fundamental question" at all, who, as they live from day to day, trust to luck it out (so to speak) and venture ahead haphazardly with frightening thoughtlessness.

How many are there, for example, who, before getting married, had reflected on St. Paul's teaching that one who, following his vocation, picks the married state, *"does well"*, but he who is not so called and for God's sake does not choose to marry, *"does better"* (I Cor. 7:38)? How many persons, who are engaged or married, were interested in determining whether God favored them with something *"better"* (in itself), namely, the consecrated vocation, instead of something merely *"good"*, namely, the vocation to marriage?

It may happen one day not far away, that they find themselves committed to an unmeaningful life and will be painfully prompted to ask themselves too late what God truly wanted of them. They will be like that good

3

old lady making a voyage who, out in the middle of the Atlantic, finally asked an officer of the vessel, "Excuse me, Sir. Is this the right ship to take for America?"

How many bitter regrets are heard from people whose sad mistake was that of choosing their path without due consideration beforehand! How many lives are ruined because people have neglected to ask themselves that "fundamental question" at a suitable time! Seneca shrewdly declared that for very many men it is true that they "spoil one part of their lives by doing evil; they spoil a greater part it by doing nothing; and they spoil the rest of it doing everything but what they should do." That is why St. Alphonsus, citing in one of his books, Fr. Granada, who described choice of a state of life as the *"chief wheel of our whole life"*, adds this wise comment: "As with a watch, when the master wheel is broken, the whole watch ceases to function, so in the order of our salvation, when the choice of a state in life is mistaken, the entire life is mistaken."

Let every boy and girl seriously reflect on this exhortation of St. Paul: *"I beseech you, brethren ... be not conformed to this world"* — be not worldly-minded; *"but be reformed in the newness of your mind, that you may prove what is the good and the acceptable and the perfect will of God"* (Rom. 12: 1-2).

We must take care, then, to ask and answer the "fundamental question" that will enable us to live a life leading us to the Kingdom of Heaven, according to the state — whatever it be — that God has determined for us. St. Augustine wrote very meaningfully, "We are living our life in vain if we are not using it to earn eternal life."

The example of St. Francis Xavier, a brilliant student at Paris, is one to remember. His ambition was to restore his noble family to its former greatness. He lived only for this. One day he met St. Ignatius Loyola, who became his roommate and classmate. From St. Ignatius young Francis heard again and again these powerful words of the Gospel, *"what does it profit a man to gain the whole world, and suffer the loss of his own soul?"* (Mt. 16: 26). At first these words left little impression on Francis. But little by little, they penetrated his heart and moved him to decide to repudiate the world with all its lures and choose God. Instead of seeking the restoration of his family, he dedicated himself to building the Kingdom of God in the souls of the faithful, as he toiled with incredible zeal in far-away Asia. He became the heavenly Patron of Catholic Missions in the Orient.

Young people who read this, consider yourselves. Do not be dazzled by the lure of creatures or by thoughtless impulses and feelings. Look ahead, look to the far future, think of eternity. "What does it profit a man to gain the whole world, and then suffer the loss of his own soul?" *(Mt. 16: 26) One indication you have of a calling is to appreciate the value of the soul you must save and sanctify, by going wherever you could best be assured your spiritual life would grow and mature to the full stature of Christ (cf. Eph. 4:13).*

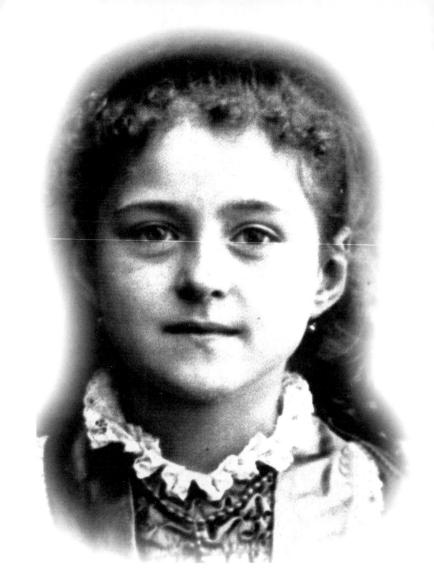

"I saw that all vocations are summend up in Love and Love is All in All!"

Photograph of St. Therérèse of the Child Jesus at age 8.

SIGNS AND IDEALS

Not infrequently, indications of a vocation appear very early, even in early childhood. We have beautiful convincing examples, as is seen in this small selection of cases compiled by a contemporary scholar. (*Father Remo di Gesù, Virtue in Examples, vol. I, p. 966 .*)

"From the time he was quite small, St. Paul of the Cross used to assemble his brothers and sisters in his home at Ovada, and then speak to them so touchingly about Our Lord's Passion that they would all be deeply moved and all eyes would be moist with tears. This was a foreshadowing of the future preacher, deeply devoted to his Crucified Lord, the religious Founder, the apostle who would convert a multitude of sinners.

"When very small, St. Teresa of Avila and other girls her age used to play at being religious Sisters. She would teach them points of meditation, the way to remain recollected, and a method for making a retreat, etc. And her little companions used to follow her directions very well. Such was the early life of the great Foundress of the reform of Carmel.

"St. Joseph Cottolengo was a small child, when his mother surprised him one day while he was measuring the length and width of the rooms in his home.

'What are you trying to do?', she asked.

'I am figuring out how many sickbeds can be put into these rooms.'

"Later on God made use of him to found the famous hospital center known as *'Little House of Providence'* in Turin.

"Who has not heard about how Napoleon, as a boy, used to make snow fortresses with his playmates and form two opposing troops for a snow-battle, and how the troop commanded by him would always win?

"As a child of four, Lacordaire used to climb up on a chair in his home and preach with such earnestness that his parents were startled and concerned. *'I can't be still!'*, he would say. *'There is too much sinning! Too much sinning!'*

"Don Louis Guanella (1915), founder of the Servants of Charity, who dedicate themselves to caring for destitute, abandoned and mentally defective people, used to play with his little sister, Catherine, gathering soil and putting it into a cavity of a rock that they had filled with water. Mixing water and earth to make a mush, they would say, *'When we grow up we will make minestra (soup) this way for the poor.'*

"At the age of seven Joseph Verdi was ecstatic on hearing a street-musician play the violin. One day he said to his parents, *'Let me study music. Don't you see what it means to me?'*

"As a child William Marconi, the famous inventor, used to spend entire days putting machinery together and taking it apart, especially electrical machines."

We can say that such children are truly fortunate, sometimes privileged above others, and as a rule, are destined for exceptional achievements or roles.

This is certainly not the case with everybody. Ordinarily, the indications of a vocation mature and gradually appear as one is growing up. The golden dreams of childhood and the bolder ones of adolescence give way to inquiry and to patient study of an ideal, of the pattern of the life one would make his own by dedicated and constant effort. How many times does one's calling prove to be the contrary of what one had expected and wanted? Consider, for example, St. Francis of Assisi, a brilliant young man, already on the road to human glory and wealth. Then, with a call from God, he was changed into a man wholly given to the Gospel, to poverty, to humility, to becoming crucified with Christ .

The father and mother of St. Thérèse of Lisieux, before they met, fell in love and married, sincerely thought they were called to the religious life in a monastery. They asked the religious superiors for admission. Their cases were thoroughly examined, and they were sent home to pursue the ordinary course of matrimony. So doing, they achieved holiness and gave the Church that heavenly flower, that little girl who became the Saint and Doctor we know as the Little Flower of Jesus.

There are examples of who persons from childhood firmly rejected the ideal of following Jesus, but for whom, later on, this ideal would become the fixed, powerful center of their lives .

Such was the case of St. Andrew Fournet. As a boy he received much encouragement from his mother to consider the priesthood and orient himself along that path. But as a kind of polite protest the boy wrote on the cover of his notebook: "I will be neither priest nor friar."

What, then, did he become? He became a brave soldier and would have continued his military career, if had he not observed within himself, as he persevered in his daily prayers and upright morals, an ever more insistent summons from God. He finally laid aside his uniform, entered upon priestly studies, and became a priest and a Saint, dying at the age of eighty after many heroic achievements that only God can count.

But in the case of sacred vocations one must be on guard against *"straw flare-ups"* of enthusiasm, of occasional and short-lasting infatuation. These often have the plausible appearance of an attractive vocation.

This is illustrated by an interesting incident in the life of St. Bernardine of Sienna before he became a Franciscan.

He had become acquainted with the Hermits of St. Augustine, and was so impressed that, overwhelmed by youthful enthusiasm, he decided to give himself to the eremitical life in their Order. But it was only a dream. In one of his sermons he speaks of it: "My desire was to live like an angel, no longer like a man.. I had in mind to live on water and vegetables, and thought about going off into a forest... And that is what I decided to do; and in order to live according to God, I decided to buy a Bible... and to try out the life I wanted to lead... I left Porta Follonica, and began by preparing myself a salad dish containing a spiny weed called sow-thistle, with other herbs. I had no bread nor salt nor oil... After blessing it in the name of Jesus, I took a spoonful of sow-thistle. Once it was in my mouth I began to chew. I chewed and chewed, and it would not go down. Being unable to swallow it, I said 'Let us drink a sip of water.'

"Oh! The water went down. But the sow-thistle stayed in my mouth. Several more sips of water, but I could not swallow the sow-thistle. Do you see my point? With the spoonful of sow-thistle, I was rid of the whole temptation— for I know it certainly was a temptation."

St. Frances Xavier Cabrini had a much different experience as a child. One day she heard a missionary tell of mission life in China. The talk enkindled missionary ideals in the child's heart, and they were imprinted there until her death. In the natural way little girls have, her behavior started showing this interest in missionary life. Her games, her sacrifices, her prayers, her whole conduct continued to give evidence of this. Like other little girls, she liked to play with dolls. But she dressed all her dolls up as nuns. She liked to play with little cardboard boats and fill them up with violets that represented missionary sisters setting out for pagan countries. When she came to know that in China, people did not have Italian candies, cookies and cakes, she decided at once to adopt the habit of not eating them any more. In her prayers she could never forget to mention the missions and beg Divine assistance for them. Thus the religious vocation of this great apostle developed with constancy and harmony from the time of her childhood.

We need, however, to avoid another extreme. Some persons, anxious to prove whether a suspected vocation is not just a dream or "straw flare-up," want always to experience an immense fascination, a great enthusiasm, a burning ardor for a vocation consecrated to God.

Let us rather heed what St. Francis de Sales wisely teaches: "To have a sign of a true vocation, it is not necessary that our sensations and feeling of love for it be constant. It is enough if our constant tendency for it be in the superior part of the soul. Therefore we must not judge that a vocation is not a true one, if the individual thus called, before taking the decisive, definitive steps, no longer experiences the happy sensations and sentimental feelings that he had in the beginning; no, not even if he might feel a distaste and coldness, which sometimes bring him to waver and make it seem like all is lost. It is enough if the will remains constant in not abandoning the Divine call and some affection for this vocation remains in our heart. To know whether God would like one to become a religious, one ought not expect that God Himself speak or send us an angel from Heaven to indicate His will. It is equally unnecessary that ten or twelve doctors of theology study the case to see whether the vocation should be followed or not. What is necessary is that one respond to the first movement of the inspiration and cultivate it, and then not grow weary if a displeasure or coldness should come on. If thus one cooperates, God will not fail to make all succeed for His glory."

Young readers, attend carefully to this: you may have some signs that God has favored and chosen you, but they are hidden under varied attractions drawing you to a career in the world. Perhaps you are waiting for extraordinary signs whereby God might summon you, whereas the Lord wants to call you in His ordinary, delicate and sweet way. Be watchful about this! Often repeat these words of St. Paul and St. Francis of Assisi: "Lord, what will you have me to do?" – and listen with your heart – a heart open unconditionally to fulfill His will.

St. Anthony of Padua when Our Lord appeared to him in a form of a Child.

"To develop the interior life fully, one must offer to God that last 'but'. This total offering, without reserve, is the condition for the complete development of the life of grace."

Photograph of St. Maximilian Mary Kolbe,
when he was a student in Rome.

THE TWO VOCATIONS

Men have two fundamental vocations — the vocation to married life and the vocation to a life consecrated to God as a priest, a religious, or a missionary.

The great St. Athanasius wrote many centuries ago: "The states of life — life's fundamental styles — are of two sorts. One is the common state, adapted to the tendencies of human living, and that state is matrimony. The other is angelic and apostolic, higher beyond comparison, and that is the state of virginity and the monastic life ."

We can certainly say, however, that the term "vocation", in the narrowest sense, expresses God's special call to the priesthood and to the religious life. That is, when one is talking about vocation, he generally means to speak of the sacred vocation. Why? For the simple reason that a calling to the married life is an *inborn, ordinary, common calling*, ingrained in man's flesh and blood. One can say it is taken for granted. People generally presume marriage will happen during man's life. The *sacred* vocation, on the other hand, requires a *special* intervention of God. It is an impulse from Heaven and directed heavenward. God, in a special way, leads the one called along the road of consecration. *"It is not given to all,"* said Our Lord, speaking expressly of the consecrated life. Rather it is given only to those whom God chooses and specially calls (Mt. 19: 11).

In the Gospel we find an example of Jesus' explicit, direct, personal call only in the case of the Apostles (*"Follow Me!"*) and the rich young man (*"Come follow Me"*), and it is always a call to consecration, a calling coming as a surprise amid the commonplace events of a life, a calling expressly willed by Our Lord: " *You have not chosen Me, but I have chosen you* " (Jn. 15: 16).

Every boy and girl, every young person, every man trying to find the right path, before choosing a state of life, ought carefully to explore which of the two fundamental vocations he has received from Our Lord. *"Give consideration to your calling,"* St. Paul admonishes us (I Cor. 1: 26).

One must not proceed thoughtlessly, whimsically, or blindly in a matter as important as choosing a state of life. St. Gregory Nazienzen was justified in saying that "once a person errs in his vocation, everything in his life is in error, everything goes badly." And St. Philip Neri wisely advises that "to choose one's state of life one needs time, counsel and prayer."

Oh, how evidently lacking in many young people is serious thought, prayer, and wise consultation, when they decide to marry someone without grasping anything at all about the great vocation and great task that couples "called" to marry one another receive from God! For this reason we see many marriages ending in tears and tragedy.

Commonly, people hardly ever go seriously into the question of whether God has happily favored them with a calling to the consecrated state. Sad to say, many who are favored, put out of their minds all possibility of being called by God to a life dedicated to Him. Many, furthermore, have even a horror and terror of finding in themselves any sacred vocation. They only care about earthly goods and about enjoying creatures in this world, and that seems enough to them. They see nothing better and allow for nothing better.

The Holy Spirit strongly admonishes young people in these words: *"I write to you, young men... the world passes away and the concupiscence thereof,"* whereas only *"he that does the will of God abides forever"* (1 Jn. 2: 14, 17).

How many young men who marry (sometimes no older than eighteen) are satisfied that they are doing God's will? How many of them, rather let themselves be conquered by lures of the flesh when they had been called by God to higher life, to a consecrated life?

St. John Bosco with his extraordinary experience in dealing with youth, could declare," A third of our young people carry the seed of a priestly and religious vocation."

How is it, then, that priests, religious, consecrated souls, are so few in the world? Evidently, great is man's failure to respond to God's call. But what will be God's judgment when so many discover that they erred about their vocation and had not even taken notice of the sublime gift of a call from God to the consecrated life?

One must put an end to false, childish prejudices against a vocation. There are fears that the priestly life and religious life is a kind of imprisonment on account of the sacred bonds whereby the creature is bound to his Lord. But unbelievably little notice is given to the far more actual and more numerous enslavements which are part of life in the world (work, family, sex, entertainment, smoking, sports...) in the service, not of God, but of Masters often anything but deserving of that service. St. Paul rightly rejoiced at being *"a prisoner of Christ."* But how could anybody rightly rejoice at being *"prisoner"* of his job, of his boss, of the foreman of his labor crew, or prisoner of material interests or of his sexual impulses?

When St. Francis of Assisi was on his way to Apulia to enter military service under Walter of Brienne, the Lord asked him, *"Francis, which is better, to become the follower of the servant or the follower of the Master?"* "The follower of the Master" answered Francis. *"And why, then, are you going to follow the servant?"*, the Lord asked. Francis understood, and at once asked, "Lord, what would You have me to do?" *"Return to Assisi,"* the Lord told him.

Let this be clear, therefore: Whoever has a Divine vocation is called to follow and serve the Master. He has been chosen by Him and is united to Him by bonds of consecration. O blessed and fruitful bonds! O bonds of pure love, of infinite love! For infinite is He who loves us and assures us, *"My yoke is sweet my burden is light"* (Mt. 11: 28-30).

If we would, we have the testimonies of two great "prisoners". One, a *prisoner of Christ,* is St. Leonard of Port Maurice, a Franciscan and a celebrated preacher. The other is a *prisoner of flesh and creatures,* and he is Wolfgang Goethe, the noted German poet.

"I am seventy-two years old, "exclaimed St. Leonard, "and I have never been unhappy, not even an hour" — in spite of the sufferings of an exhausting, trying apostolate.

"I am seventy-two years old," Wolfgang Goethe declared, "and I have never had one hour of happiness" — although he had his full share of worldly delights and carnal pleasure.

Another humble, holy Franciscan, St. Seraphin of Montegranaro, put it well: *"I will not give one inch of my cord"* — the sash cord (symbolizing servitude to Christ) of the Franciscan habit — *"in exchange for all goods of this world."* St. Bernardine of Sienna explains why: *"When a soul starts relishing Jesus, he necessarily finds the world distasteful."* But the inspired psalmist had once sung and prophesied to the people of his day, *"O taste, and see that the Lord is sweet"* (33: 9). *"How lovely are Your tabernacles, O Lord of Hosts!"* (83: 1) *"Blessed are they that dwell in Your house, O Lord. They shall praise You forever and ever"* (83: 5).

Young people, take care not to err!

"The vocation" Pope Paul VI said, "is a grace not given to everybody. But it can be, even today, given to many: to many strong and pure young people, to many souls longing for a higher beauty in their life, longing for perfection, with a passion for the salvation of their fellow man.

"We pray that it be so. Is there perhaps someone listening to our humble talk now, who hears within him Jesus' majestic voice?

"Let us pray that it be so. Our blessing is upon all who 'hear the word of God and keep it.'"

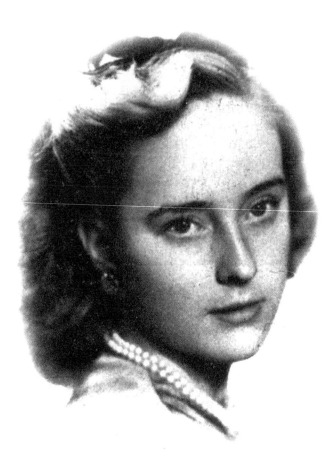

"O Mary, may all who look at me, see You!"

Photograph of Ven. Maria Teresa Quevedo,
before her entrance to the convent.
A young spanish Carmelite
who died at the age of 20.

THE GREATEST GIFT

When the Apostles bluntly remarked to Jesus that if married life involves such heavy obligations as unity and indissolubility, it is better not to marry, Jesus replied without mincing words, that a life consecrated to God is not possible for everybody, but only for *"those to whom it is given"* (Mt. 19: 11).

The vocation to a life consecrated for the Kingdom of Heaven is, therefore, a special gift, a personal gift, a privileged gift granted by God not to the majority, but to the minority. No one can bestow this privilege on himself, for Jesus said, *"You have not chosen Me, but I have chosen you"* (Jn. 15: 16).

St. Paul would have preferred all men to live in the state of consecration to God — the state in which he lived. He dared to write, *"Are you unmarried?... do not seek to get married"* (I Cor. 7: 27). And elsewhere he adds that the married state is *"good"*, but remaining single and pure *"is better"* (I Cor. 7: 38). Why? Because in a life of chaste virginity, one's heart is *"undivided"* in loving God, in seeking His pleasure, and in dedicating oneself to Divine things by keeping oneself *"holy both in body and spirit"* (I Cor. 7: 34).

Yet, St. Paul himself had to conclude that *"everyone should remain in that vocation to which he had been called"* (I Cor. 7: 20); for the noblest gifts are not for all, but only for those *"whom He Himself [God] chooses"* (Mk. 3: 13).

Our Lord, moreover, extolled the gift of a vocation to the consecrated life of virginity as an aspect of paradise, a treasure of the Kingdom of Heaven, a foretaste in this world of the life of Heaven, an incarnation of an angelic life on earth: *"The children of this world marry and are given in marriage; but... the children of the Resurrection... are like the angels of God"* (cf. Lk. 20: 34-36).

Hence, St. Ambrose had good reason to say, "If the blessed Spirits are the virgins of Heaven, the virgins are the angels on earth." Again he says, "Virginity, which makes man like the angels, is that which is loveliest in human nature. But in the virgins there is something not found in the angels; namely, angels have no body, while in virgins it is precisely the body that becomes their instrument of victory." St. Cyprian adds, "O virgins, safeguard what you are and safeguard what you shall be... You already have in this world a glory of the Resurrection."

The reality of the sublime grace of a life consecrated to God, the grace of a religious life consists in this: creatures become *"like the angels of God in Heaven"* (Mt. 22: 30). We see this angelic quality clearly in figures like St. Francis of Assisi, St. Clare, St. Anthony, St. Catherine, St. Aloysius, St. Bernadette, St. John Bosco, the Little Flower, St. Gemma, St. Maximilian Maria Kolbe... Oh what *"brilliance of eternal light"* (Wis. 7: 26) shines in these figures of our brothers and sisters consecrated to Jesus!

Therefore, whoever has the exalted gift of a religious vocation should not hesitate to leave all, to be consecrated to God, that is, to give himself to Jesus entirely, with *"undivided heart"* for the practice of holiness *"of body and spirit"* (I Cor. 7:34).

Jesus, Himself, assures us that whoever, for God's sake, *"leaves his family... will have eternal life as his inheritance"* (Mt. 19: 29).

Whoever consecrates himself to God, whoever gives himself to Jesus, forsaking all for His sake, is like one who leaves appearances for reality, according to St. Paul's words: visible goods (home, employment, father, mother...) pass away, while invisible goods (God, grace, souls the Kingdom of Heaven) are everlasting realities.

When St. Francis of Assisi succeeded in ridding himself of all his earthly goods and of all creatures— even breaking from his father— he could exclaim in holy fervor, *"My God and my all!"* He had been freed from every creature, and now he possessed what was his All. Such is the religious life. Such is the state of consecrated persons living in monasteries and convents, in hermitages and religious houses.

St. Basil comments, "In this privileged state there is a happy and wonderful exchange; for goods of this world are given up and in their place the goods of Heaven are received. Treasures that will pass away are surrendered in exchange for treasures that last forever. Articles of no value are swapped for articles of priceless value." The holy Doctor, St. Augustine, confesses that "human speech cannot pay worthy honor to the religious life. Whenever I try to do it," he adds, "I feel compelled to keep silent; for I am incapable of paying tribute to a life so sublime and angelic."

We need, moreover to meditate on another reality of grace linked to consecrated virginity; namely, every virgin soul so consecrated becomes a *"bride to Christ,"* as the liturgy of the Church chants. Jesus, Himself, is called Bridegroom of prudent virgins in the parable of the ten virgins (cf. Mt. 25:1 ff.) The Prophet Isaiah wrote in his day, *"Indeed, ...as a young man weds a virgin, so your Creator will wed Himself to you. As the bridegroom delights in his bride, so your God will delight in you"* (Is. 62:5).

Virginity and Divine nuptials, virginity and Divine joy, virginity and spiritual maternity — these all go together. The angelic St. Thérèse of Lisieux wrote these beautiful lines; *"To be Your spouse, O Jesus, is to become a mother of souls through union with You."* Oh, the heavenly charm of a life of consecrated virginity!

The Church has always taught this. In his splendid encyclical *Sacra Virginitas* and his discourses to consecrated souls, Pius XII wonderfully expounded these themes. He calls consecrated virgins *"true spouses of the Lord,"* following here the ancient Church Fathers, who considered holy virgins to be *"spouses of Christ"* in the truest and highest sense. St. Methodius of Olympus, for example, composed this prayer for a consecrated virgin: *"O Christ, for me You are everything. For Your sake I remain pure, and with lamp brightly burning, I come to meet You, O my Bridegroom."*

At this point I believe we would not think the Carmelite mystic, St. Mary Magdeline di Pazzi, to exaggerate when she declares, "A religious vocation is the greatest grace God can give a soul after holy Baptism."

Nor is Blessed Orione going too far when he writes, "I would count it a great favor if Jesus would grant me to go about the streets begging to the very last moment of my life in exchange for vocations."

These inspired words of Pope Pius XII on our subject should be meditated on by Christian parents: "If God should some day, do you the great honor of seeking one of your sons or daughters for His service, know how to appreciate how precious, how privileged is such a grace for your son or daughter, for you and your family. It is a great gift from Heaven that has come to your home..."

One day, the father of the Little Flower, St. Thérèse, heard his daughter Celine remark that she, too, wanted to consecrate herself entirely to Jesus to live the life of a virgin of Carmel. Deeply moved, he said to her, "Come, let us thank Our Lord in the Blessed Sacrament for the favors He is granting our family and the honor He is doing me by picking His spouses from my home! Yes! The good God does me a great honor by taking my daughters away for Himself."

You young people who read these lines, look into your hearts, recollect yourselves in prayer, be not deaf to God's voice. Jesus may have chosen you, loved you, called you – indeed is calling you! "Come, follow Me!" (Mt. 19:21) – and would bestow on you His greatest gift which would make you like "an angel of God in Heaven" (Mt. 22: 30).

"What must I tell you? You too have come into the world as I have, with a mission to accomplish..."

Photograph of Bl. Padre Pio of Pietrelcina, the only priest who bore the stigmata.

PRIEST OF JESUS

If the religious life is angelic, *"like the angels of God in Heaven"* (Mt. 22: 30), the priestly life ought to be considered more than angelic, for the priest has the power and the mission to do what even angels cannot do. Except for God, no one but the priest has the power and the commission to change bread and wine into Our Lord's Body and Blood and forgive the sins of all repentant sinners.

With the priesthood, man surpasses the heights of created power and greatness. He enters the realm of the uncreated, of the Divine, even of the Divine Person of Jesus. He becomes, as it were, Jesus who transubstantiates the bread and wine, who takes away sin from every soul, who instructs, who guides and brings to salvation.

Is it not, perhaps, on this account, that the priest is venerated even by his guardian angel, who stands at his left instead of at his right, to give the priest precedence as St. Francis de Sales assures us?

The priest reproduces Jesus, continues and prolongs Our Lord's saving mission. He shares the same Paschal Mystery of Jesus: crucifixion and Resurrection.

So Jesus spoke to His first priests: *"Come, and I will make you fishers of men..."* (Mt. 4: 19). *"As the Father has sent Me, I also send you"* (Jn. 20: 21). *"Take... This is My Body... This is the chalice of My Blood"* (Mt. 26: 26). *"Whose sins you shall forgive, they are forgiven them: and whose sins you shall retain, they are retained"* (Jn. 20: 23). *"Going, therefore, teach all nations"* (Mt. 28: 19). *"He that hears you hears Me: and he that despises you, despises Me"* (Lk. 10: 16). *"If they have persecuted Me, they will also persecute you"* (Jn. 15: 20). *"You are not of the world, as I also am not of the world... therefore the world hates you"* (Jn. 17: 14; 15: 19).

We cannot but be bewildered when we reflect on the superhuman reality of the priesthood. We perhaps can glimpse it recalling how St. Francis of Assisi— that seraphic, heavenly man— had not the courage or the boldness to accept ordination to the priesthood and chose to remain a deacon. In the history of the holy Church Fathers, we learn that St. Ephrem, Doctor of the Church, chose never to be more than a deacon; and that St. Augustine wept bitterly the day of his priestly ordination; that St. John Chrysostom and St. Ambrose went into hiding in a futile effort to avoid being obliged to accept the office of bishop.

In her famous *Dialogues,* St. Catherine of Sienna referred to priests when she wrote that one day Eternal Wisdom told her, "Open the eyes of your mind and contemplate Me, who am the Sun of Righteousness. Then you will see the ministers in glory who, having directed their aim and gaze to this Sun, have taken on the condition of the Sun!"

St. John Vianney, the holy Curé of Ars, used to say that if God were to enlighten people on the value of priesthood, no one would dare receive priestly ordination. Likewise, if men were well aware of the value of the Holy Mass, the priest would not have the venturesomeness to celebrate it, nor would our people dare assist at it. The holy Curé used to try to explain it this way : "All good works put together are not worth as much as the Sacrifice of the Mass; for they are works of man, whereas the Mass is the work of God. Compared to it, even martyrdom is nothing. Martyrdom is the sacrifice of man to God, while in the Mass, God is sacrificed for man!"

To celebrate Holy Mass, to forgive sins, to administer the Body and Blood of Christ to souls, to pass on to all men the bread of God's word— all this constitutes a mission of supreme importance to the entire Mystical Body of Christ. Even the last and least known priest on earth— as St. John Vianney may seem to have been when he set out for the village of Ars— is a worker of great wonders when he dispenses *"the Divine mysteries"* (I Cor. 4: 1) and gives increase to the vitality of the members of the *"Body of Christ, which is the Church."* (Col. 1: 24)

We can truthfully apply to every priest these Divine words of the Psalmist : *"I will give You the Gentiles for Your inheritance, and the out most parts of the earth for Thy possession"* (Ps. 2: 8). And so it is. Two recent examples bear out the truth of these words. Has not St. Maximilian Maria Kolbe, a humble, ardent son of St. Francis, become priestly hero loved and honored all over the world? Did he not establish two marvelous citadels of the Immaculate Virgin, one in Poland and one in Japan? Has Pope John Paul II not proclaimed him *"Special protector of our times"?* And Blessed Padre

Pio of Pietrelcina, a no less humble, ardent son of St. Francis— has his following not been *"worldwide"*, as Pope Paul VI declared? As he toiled, suffered and prayed in his friary on Mt. Gargano, did the people not *"come to him from everywhere"?* (Mt. 1: 45). And is he not the inspired founder of two wonderful projects— a vast medical center and hospital called Home for the Relief of Suffering, and an organization of Prayer Groups? The most superhuman powers, the most sublime realities, exist in the heart and hands of every priest.

Here is something on the priesthood written in his diary by a holy priest of our time, Don Joseph Canovai, who died at the age of thirty four: "I find myself shuddering and my heart throbbing at the immense, august, heavenly power of the priesthood. I feel it surpassing the limits of my soul and reaching to Heaven, as it bestows the peace of pardon and the word of life. I see it wielding its power even to the threshold of death, where He who is Mercy Itself, having spent Himself on the Cross, brings salvation.

"The priesthood, like an ancient tree with its branches in the Heavens, grows at the foot of the Cross from the soil watered by the Blood of Christ; and the souls that are redeemed become the joys of priestly life."

Priests are the most indispensable creatures on earth, the most salutary and blessed. No matter how frail and burdened with defects, they have always the power to give grace, to give men the bread of eternal life and to bring them God's Word, to comfort the sick, to give support and hope to the dying, to enlighten and guide men who go astray. Without grace, without the Eucharist, without God's Word, how can we live uprightly and gain eternal salvation?

"Let a town be without a priest for twenty years," the Holy Curé of Ars used to say with good reason, "and the people will start adoring animals."

It is true, so true that there can be no greater misfortune or worse punishment for a nation or for a diocese than for the number of worthy priests to dwindle. There can be no greater calamity for Christendom and for society than having too few worthy priests. Failure of the people to perceive this truth is a sign that the process of dechristianization is sailing ahead, blinding men, obscuring all worthy ideals, especially in young people, who prefer to belong to big herds of restless idlers rather than to ask themselves seriously if they are not called by the Lord to a field more fruitful and valuable: the field of God's Kingdom in his brethren, especially in the poorest people, the oppressed, the despairing.

It is very painful to realize how many idle young people are wasting away in unhappiness and boredom. They could be able bearers of God to men, bearers of men to God, and bearers of God Himself. "The priesthood," writes St. Ephrem brilliantly, "functions in the Church like a flight of eagles as they quit the earth and boldly rise toward God. In their powerful claws they carry men's sacred offerings and lay them at the foot of the throne of the Divine Majesty. From thence, they carry back to earth God's sacred favors to sanctify the souls that would approach the venerable Mysteries of which the priest is the dispenser."

May the youthful readers of these lines reflect on these facts: In Italy in the nineteenth century, with several million inhabitants less than today, there were over 150,000 priests. In Italy today, with several million more inhabitants, priests number a little less than 30,000. Evident consequences of this are the atheism wide spread among the people, the frightful decline in the worthy reception of the sacraments, the most crass ignorance of true religion, the giant increase that moral corruption is taking and the legalizing of degrading, murderous practices, such as divorce, abortion and drug trafficking.

You young persons reading these lines, pause and reflect. True "workers for the harvest" are lacking. Enter within yourself. Pray, and listen — listen to Our Lord. Perhaps He is calling you, choosing you, and wishes to make you "the salt of the earth and light of the world" (Mt. 5: 13), "fishers of men" (Mk. 1: 17). Perhaps, as you ponder these pages, you may hear it said within your heart, "The Master is here and He is calling you" (Jn. 11: 28).

WHOM MIGHT JESUS CALL?

"Father, I want to be a sister."

"Oh, fine! You of all people, Maria Bertilla! Isn't it so that you are not very good at anything?"

"But I will try to do something."

"Drop the idea, my little dumpling! How could you want them to make a sister out of you?"

This was her first approach to her pastor when Maria Bertilla Boscardin revealed her vocation to become a sister.

But a few days later the pastor, troubled by misgivings, sent for Maria Bertilla and asked her, "Tell me honestly, do you really want to become a sister?"

"Yes, Father."

"Do you truly feel that Jesus calls you to belong to Him as a bride forever?"

"Yes, Father."

"Now, can you at least peel potatoes?"

"Yes, Father."

"Then I want you to go over to the convent to peel the potatoes."

In this way Maria Bertilla was able to join the Dorothean Sisters. And this poor *"little dumpling"*, having got her start peeling potatoes, became the glorious St. Bertilla, a woman of heroic humility and sincerity, whose life was one of heroic self-sacrifice.

If this example provokes us to ask, *"Whom might Jesus call?"* we should answer that He might call anybody; for there is no category of persons which excludes the grace of a vocation to a consecrated life. The Lord knows us all and can call whomever He wills. *"He counts the number of the stars and calls each by name"* (Ps. 146: 4).

The Holy Gospels tell us that those whom Jesus called included young men and older men, fishermen and day-laborers, white-collar workers and unemployed job-seekers.

St. John the Evangelist was just a youth. St. Peter had reached full adulthood. Both were fishermen. St. Matthew was a clerk in a tax office. St. Paul worked as a tent-maker. Then we should remember the jobless whom the Lord of the vineyard asked at the eleventh hour, *"Why stand you here all the day idle?"* And their vocation came at that late hour, as Our Savior says in the parable (Mt. 20: 1-16).

Down the centuries of Christian history, Jesus has called to His following both boys and older men, both men and women, people of blameless reputation as well as sinners, from among all classes of society.

The call came during their childhood to St. Benedict, St. Thomas Aquinas, St. Aloysius Gonzaga, St. Pius X, St. Maximilian Maria Kolbe, St. Agnes, St. Bernadette, and the Little Flower.

St. Anthony of Padua was a teenager, as were St. Gerard Majella, St. Gabriel of the Sorrowful Mother, St.

John Berchman, St. John Bosco, St. Catherine of Sienna, St. Veronica Juliani, and St. Maria Bertilla.

During early manhood and maidenhood God called St. Anthony the Abbot, St. Bernard, St. Francis of Assisi, St. Francis Xavier, St. Alphonsus Liguori, St. Scholastica, St. Clare, St. Margaret Mary Alacoque.

In adulthood God called the Apostles (except St. John), St. Augustine, St. Ignatius of Loyola, St. Camillus de Lellis, St. Mary Magdalene, St. Mary of Egypt, St. Margaret of Cortona, Bl. Angela of Foligno.

Our Lord will not be overruled by anyone. He calls with sovereign love and freedom. He calls whomever He wills, when He wills, and as He wills.

It is He alone who *"has determined some to be Apostles, and some to be Prophets, others to be Evangelists, others to be Pastors and Doctors"* (Eph. 4: 11).

It is He who called some to become outstanding Popes, like St. Gregory the Great and St. Leo the Great, or great doctors of the Church, like St. Thomas Aquinas and St. Bonaventure. Others He has called to become humble and saintly friars, like St. Felix and St. Crispin. God has called little girls to become inspired Foundresses, like St. Teresa of Avila and St. Jane Antida, or to become Sisters whose lives reached an angelic sweetness, like St. Bernadette and St. Maria Bertilla.

If we would discover where Jesus' preferences lie, we would say He prefers the humble, the unlearned, the weak, according to St. Paul's teaching that *"there are not many wise according to the flesh, not many mighty, not many noble"* (I Cor. 1: 26).

But it is chiefly in the hearts of children and adolescents that God ordinarily deposits the seed of vocation; for "at the age of twelve sublime and generous ideals take hold of people," according to Alphonse Gratry, " which at the age of forty they no longer appreciate."

In a discourse on vocations, Pope John Paul II declared that "God calls everyone for a mission. He calls at any age. In a special way He calls youth;" and with emphasis he continued: "Young people, it is now your hour. It is up to you to respond. Life is God's gift. If Christ calls you to be His co-worker, do not hesitate an instant to accept generously. If I speak to you of total consecration to God in the priesthood, in the religious life, in the missionary life, it is because Christ is calling many among you to this extraordinary venture!"

Some splendid examples in our day confirm even more the fact that God is calling today's youth to a life consecrated to Him.

St. Maximilian Maria Kolbe, a shining light of Franciscan and Marian holiness, was a little more than twelve years old when he took private tutoring in order to continue his schooling. One day, hearing a sermon, he learned that a Franciscan seminary had opened for boys hoping to be followers of St. Francis of Assisi. Enlightened by grace, he at once asked to be admitted. He was accepted, entered upon his studies, made progress, and became a son of St. Francis, a chivalrous lover of the Immaculate and martyr of charity at the death-camp of Auschwitz, where he offered his life in 1941 to save the father of a family.

Blessed Padre Pio of Pietrelcina, another Franciscan giant of holiness, during a sermon he heard at the age of ten felt the urge to consecrate himself to God. He, too, took private schooling in order to be able to enter the Capuchin novitiate at the age of fifteen. He became so much like the Seraphic Father St. Francis as to be sealed with the sacred stigmata of Our Lord, which he bore for fifty years until his death in 1968.

Of one young maiden, who was a jewel of sweetness, Santina Campana, we can say that from the time of her Baptism she advanced so much in her program of "all for Jesus" that she is rightly likened to the Little Flower and St. Gemma Galgani. Her religious vocation blossomed like a lily with its strong fragrance. At eighteen, as a novice, she was as devout and ingenuous as an angel. But she did not complete her novitiate until she was in paradise. After three years of intense suffering, her life ended in 1950 like a flickering sentinel, *keeping watch beside the Cross.*

Considering Our Lord's fondness for young people, let us add that one finds in them a generosity and zeal not observable in the later stages of life. They know how to practice the generosity of total love. They know how to be courageous to the point of heroism. Certainly, when they are practicing sincerity and constancy, they do not like or allow halfway measures or compromises in being faithful to the call of love. They clearly realize that great, strong love is bound up with great and hard sacrifice. Jesus loved us to the extent of making a total, bloody offering of Himself. And what do we do...?

We read in a clerical review that once "a Carmelite Mother Superior was telling a group of young Japanese converts about life within the Carmelite Order — the considerable time devoted to prayer, the severe fasts, the rugged way of life..."

Those girl's eyes were bright with joy.

But at one point the Mother Superior remarked that the severe Carmelite rule would be relaxed a little for them, seeing they were not used to such penances.

The brightness disappeared from those young eyes, as they looked at one another very disappointed.

Then one mustered her courage and spoke for them all, "Mother, we would be so happy to follow the Rule without relaxing it, because we want to practice much love for Our Lord."

Knowing that our youth often have the grace to think this way, Pope Paul VI put these questions to a group of young people: "Children, do you know that Christ needs you? Do you know that His call is addressed to the strong, to those who rebel against halfway measures and against the cowardice of a comfortable and unmeaningful life?"

Let the young reader seriously reflect: Are you, too, perhaps being called by Jesus? Would you prefer creature comforts and the lures of the world to Christ's call? Do not be slow to see the true values. Who can love you more, the Creator or the creature? If Jesus is calling you, then within your heart you are to possess the Infinite Good as your property and your wealth.

WHAT DOES IT MEAN TO FOLLOW JESUS?

To follow Jesus in the consecrated life means to live Jesus' life, which is a life that is *virginal, poor, and obedient*. It is a life of dedication to God, which is above all lived in places dedicated to Him, namely, seminaries, monasteries, friaries, religious houses for men or for women.

St. Benedict and St. Teresa of Avila, St. Gerard and St. Bernadette, lived Jesus' life in their respective religious houses, after having left, for Jesus' sake, all that they had— all things whatsoever.

Holy diocesan priests have done likewise, who did not live in religious houses, but imitated Christ in their wonderful life of virtue. Such men, for example, were the Holy Curé of Ars, St. Joseph Cafasso and St. Pius X.

The call of a religious or consecrated person to follow Jesus is not something vague and undetermined. This "following of Jesus" means putting into practice the imitation of the God-Man who was a virgin, who was poor, who was obedient unto death. It means *"to live Christ"*—to live by Him completely, by Him only, by Him exclusively.

In the life of St. Paul of the Cross we read that as a zealous, pure youth he had hard battles to fight to defend his vocation *to follow Christ*.

There was a struggle when an uncle, who was a parish priest, wanted him to marry and promised him, for his compliance, that he would inherit all his property. The priest had found a beautiful, upright and wealthy bride for him. Of one mind with the priest, the Saint's family presented the lovely maiden to be his fiancée, hoping he would finally yield and agree to the marriage.

But young Paul had no intention of turning aside, for the sake of a creature, from his decision *to follow Christ* with an undivided heart. Feeling his constancy might be imperiled, he clung fast to his Crucified Lord with fervent prayers and tears. When his uncle one day chose to take him to visit the young lady, Paul remembered the example of St. Francis de Sales; and in the girl's presence he kept his eyes cast down and remained silent and absorbed in earnest prayer.

The uncle died, and indeed the will left all his property to Paul on condition that he marry. Paul at once signed documents renouncing all title to the inheritance, taking only the breviary in order to recite the prayer of the Church. Impressive on that occasion was his prayer expressing his will to forsake everything in order to follow Christ and possess Him alone: *"O my Crucified Lord, I protest that I want nothing else of this inheritance but this breviary. You alone are enough for me. You alone will be my love now and forever."*

Something even more dramatic of this sort occurred in St. Francis of Assisi's life. A brilliant spirited youth, he had set out from Assisi on his way to Apulia to fight under the banner of Walter of Brienne, hoping to earn knighthood and place among the nobility.

But at Spoleto Francis had a vision. He heard this crucial question put to him:

"Francis, Francis, which is better, to follow the servant or the Master?"

Francis had no hesitation about answering,

"To follow the Master."

"Then why," continued the voice, *"are you leaving the Master to follow the servant?"*

Francis then saw the light, and responded,

"Lord, what will You have me to do?"

Just what does it mean to "follow Jesus"? It means to *follow the Master* rather than the servant. Any man, whoever he be, can be no more than a "servant" compared to the "Creator". Thus one can see the infinite difference between dedicating oneself and binding oneself to the service of a servant, and dedicating and binding oneself to serve our "Lord" and "Creator".

Once a good mother of a family spoke these words to her adolescent daughter, "Daughter, if you consecrate yourself to Jesus, you will be the bride of Jesus. If you marry a man, you will serve a man." This is the language of Christian wisdom. Every youth and every girl ought to grasp this truth before deciding his or her future. All young persons ought to put to themselves the fundamental question, *"Is it better to follow the servant or to follow the Master?"* Is it better to give ourselves to a creature or to the Creator? Is it better to follow a man or to follow Jesus?

In the life of St. Vincent Mario Strambi we read that as a young man he one day approached his father to tell him of his decision to enter the Passionists. He said, *"Father, I want to take my inheritance."*

The father was surprised at words so strange, both because Vincent was his only son and because there was no reason to justify such a remark. Hence he told his son that, as he was the only heir, the whole family patrimony was already his exclusively.

But Vincent was not through, and repeated, *"Father, I want my inheritance."* However, as he said these words, he knelt before a Crucifix and said, *"Father, this is the inheritance that I want to take. I want to have no inheritance but Him, my crucified Jesus. I only want to follow Him, to live and to die for Him."*

His father was consoled at this and wept. He then embraced his son and exhorted him to take hold of that inheritance to follow Jesus in life and in death.

Let us also reflect that many, many girls full of life and grace, and sometimes talented and wealthy, have generously renounced everything in order to "follow Christ", to belong totally to Christ with *"undivided"* heart, soul and body, truly angelic, virgin spouses of the Incarnate Word.

For instance, we can mention St. Veronica Juliani, who zealously struggled against the lure of her family's material goods and the attraction of creatures which strove to turn her away from "following Christ". The men who sought her hand pursued her all the way to the gate of the cloister in a last attempt to win her. There the dauntless girl turned and cast aside the bouquet of flowers she was carrying, exclaiming, *"These flowers that quickly wither are for you — for the world that is so seductive!"*

This virgin, so rich in grace, gave herself entirely to Jesus in order to become one with Him. She reached a mystical stage of suffering, a bloody crucifixion of soul and body for the salvation of souls. For long years she bore Christ's stigmata—Christ's wounds—on her body, which was crucified for love of her Crucified Lover.

Those chosen to *"follow Jesus"* are called to such ideals of Divine Love, to such lofty heights.

And what can be nobler during this earthly life? In Jesus is found the fullness of life, of perfection and of holiness. Whoever follows Him by living that same Divine life of virginity, of poverty, and of obedience, can reach a fullness of Divine life with every perfection and holiness. Take just a glance, for example, at St. Francis of Assisi, at St. Clare, St. Catherine Laboure, St. Aloysius, St. Alphonsus, St. John Bosco.

Lord Jesus, how much we ought to thank You for having called so many to follow You! How much gratitude we owe You for continuing to call many to Your following without considering such things as merits or other qualifications. You choose souls because You wish to give man the honor of imitating You more fully. And we know that You call many in spite of the failure of so many to respond. How tragic! Men prefer to follow the guidance of another creature rather than *"follow Jesus"*! Yes, some men prefer to live a sad human existence, following the ordinary way of creatures, rather than to live Jesus' life, to imitate Him and to reproduce His life, as did St. Francis of Assisi and all the other Saints. O Lord, what folly! But keep calling men, we beg You.

Young reader, pay careful attention. The fundamental question that transformed young Francis into the glorious St. Francis of Assisi – "Lord, what would You have me to do?" – *is also the question you must ask. Do not evade this question; for it will always hold true that only* "by serving God does one reign." *If Jesus chooses to call you to* "follow Him" *in order to let you* "reign with Him", *even in this world, it would be madness to desire not to know of it, preferring ignorance about it so that you may give yourself over to serve the creature, when you know well how vain are the sons of men;* "the sons of men are liars in the balance: that by vanity they may together deceive" (Ps. 61:10).

But to "follow Our Lord" *is to follow* Him *who is* "the Way, the Truth, and the life." (Jn. 14: 6)

Photograph of Ven. Augustus Czartoryski, a Polish prince. He joined the Salesians after overcoming much opposition, even from Queen Isabella of Spain, his Aunt.

WHY DOES JESUS CALL CERTAIN ONES TO FOLLOW HIM?

Jesus calls out of love.

Jesus loves with an infinite love. He is infinitely happy because He is Infinite Love. He desires that we, too, attain to His infinite happiness, as St. Bernard declares.

But how does one attain to this happiness of Divine Love except by possessing Divine Love in a life fully given to unreserved and total love?

This is why Jesus calls *"His own"* to follow Him along the way of a virginal and total love that does not hold back. This way is His own life, His own Personality. It is Jesus Himself — *"I am the way"* (Jn. 14: 6).

Therefore to consecrate oneself to Jesus means to love and imitate Him perfectly, copying Him in such wise as to be transformed into Him, as it were, to be identified with Him.

We should have the mind of St. Paul when he ventured to say, *"For me to live is Christ"* (Phil. 1: 21), and *"It is no longer I who live, but Christ lives in me"* (Gal. 2: 20).

Our mind should be that of St. Francis of Assisi, who so closely followed and conformed himself to Jesus, that he came to resemble his Crucified Lord physically. And like St. Francis were St. Veronica Juliani, St. Gemma

Galgani, and Blessed Padre Pio of Pietrelcina. In fact every Saint is a perfect copy of Jesus, as is evidenced, for example, in many episodes from the lives of St. Catherine Laboure and St. John Vianney.

It once happened to St. Anthony of Padua to appear with the ardent, tormented features of his Crucified Savior, causing fright in all who saw him. Those features of the Crucified Savior, revealed outwardly during those short moments, how St. Anthony had become inwardly transfigured and conformed to Our Lord, *"being made conformable to His death"* (Phil. 3: 10).

To live in virginal purity as Christ did, to be poor with Christ, to be obedient with His obedience— such is the call to religious life, to a life of Divine Love, to be lived in the radical and total way that the God-Man lived it, whom we all ought to imitate. This imitation, this conformity, is our sublime destiny willed by the heavenly Father— *"to be made conformable to the image of His Son"* (Rom. 8: 29).

If, then, the Lord calls men to the priesthood, those chosen become priests like Jesus— *other Christs*, with His Divine powers to consecrate, to administer and communicate grace, to dispense Divine mysteries, to announce the Word of God.

How great, how powerful is the love of Jesus when He chooses and calls His consecrated ones! Only love explains the existence on this earth of religious life and the priesthood. Every other explanation will always depend on this. And the response of those called ought likewise, to be primarily the response of a love that is grateful and generous, ardent and faithful.

However, sad to say, in our days especially it must be admitted that there are many defections from the consecrated life. Yes, not only are vocations fewer, but many consecrated souls have abandoned their consecration to God. We cannot hide the fact that there has been a wholesale withdrawal of consecrated persons from their priestly or their religious vocation. On those whom Our Lord had truly called, these frightening words of His shall weigh heavily: *"No man, putting his hand to the plow and looking back, is fit for the Kingdom of Heaven"* (Lk. 9: 62). The devil, the world, the flesh— man's three mortal enemies— have prevailed over an impressive number of consecrated souls, causing great scandal and distress among the faithful.

Usually the first reaction to the scandal of a consecrated soul turning traitor to Christ's love is one of severe and harsh criticism. The critic may even curse, and suffer his faith to be so shaken that he threatens to forsake it.

But this reaction is quite wrong. Why so? Because, first of all, we ought to criticize and examine ourselves. Hearing harsh criticisms against a stray priest, St. Nicholas of Flue, Patron of Switzerland, made this courageous, loyal comeback, *"As for you, how often have you prayed for the holiness of priests?... And tell me, what have you done to obtain worthy vocations for the Church?"*

One could also react with the response given by the celebrated orator and statesman, Donato Cortes, to someone who had spoken of defections among priests: "I see an immense throng of souls faithful at the price of shedding their blood. And I refuse to lose

47

confidence in the Apostles by reason of there being a Judas among them."

Moreover, consider how consecrated souls are the most valuable part of the whole Church, because Jesus has called them to be the backbone of His mystical Body. Without them the Church, in the present order of Providence, cannot stand up. Hence, we all are bound to lend them our hand with our prayers and sacrifices, that they may not fail us, may not be wanting, and may always be there to guide and help us to salvation, that there may always be such worthy ministers and religious to be *"the salt of the earth and the light of the world"* (Mt. 5: 13).

The famous Bing Crosby, when he had become a fervent Catholic, once wrote an article expressing his convictions and his loyal, courageous faith. "In my book these are my stars," he wrote. "They are the *Priest*, the *Sister*, the *Religious*. They are who make history. As for us movie people of Hollywood, we do our business and earn our money. After a little time we are gone and the money disappears, and not a thing remains of us. But these (my stars) build spiritual kingdoms, they raise up and reinforce the ideas that influence generations for many years."

A little girl enters a church with her mother, sees a large grillwork and hears the nuns praying in choir. She asks her mother, "What are the nuns doing?" The mother answers, "The nuns are praying for us so that we will not take the wrong way, but will take the road that leads us to Paradise."

She answered well. Consecrated men and women chosen by Our Lord lead the way to the Kingdom of

Heaven. If *they* grow faint, if *they* do not want to "follow Jesus" anymore, then we will find ourselves getting scattered like *"sheep without a shepherd."* (Mt. 6: 34), in serious danger of getting lost far from the way to salvation.

To achieve a *"supreme love for God"* — something Vatican II teaches — and with this love for God to labor for the upbuilding of the Church and the eternal salvation of our fellow man — this is the purpose for which Christ calls some to follow Him more perfectly along a path that is intimately entrusted and specially reserved just for the ones of His choice whom *"He Himself willed"* to be chosen (Mk. 3: 13).

These chosen ones have carried out, in the Church and for the Church, the task assigned them of incarnating Jesus according to His various perfections and dignities. For example:

Jesus, High Priest, in St. Peter and in St. PiusX;

Jesus the Good Shepherd, in St. Alphonsus Liguori;

Jesus priest, in the Holy Curé of Ars;

Jesus teacher, in St. Augustine and St. Thomas Aquinas;

Jesus preacher, in St. Anthony and St. Bernardine;

Jesus the contemplative, in St. Bernard and St. Teresa of Avila;

Jesus caring for the sick, in St. Camillus and St. Maria Bertilla;

Jesus among children, in St. John Bosco and St. Mary Mazzarello;

Jesus ministering to the poor, in St. Vincent de Paul and Blessed Louis Orione;

Jesus forgiving sins, in St. Leopold Mandic and Blessed Padre Pio of Pietrelcina;

Jesus loving His Mother, in St. Louis Grigon de Montfort and St. Maximilian Maria Kolbe;

Jesus loving the Church, in St. Gregory VII and St. Catherine of Sienna.

Let the young reader of these pages reflect in his heart. Do you not love the perfection of love? Now where will you find it? Certainly not in any creature, with all its frailty and limitations. Listen to Our Lord as He says, "If you will be perfect, go sell what you have... Come follow Me" (Mt. 19: 21). *Consider deeply these Divine words. The Apostles hearkened to them, and after their time the Saints have done likewise in every age – St. Benedict and St. Scholastica, St. Bernard and St. Gertrude, St. Francis and St. Clare, St. Anthony and St. Catherine, St. Ignatius and St. Teresa of Jesus, St. John Bosco and St. Bernadette, down to St. Maximilian Maria Kolbe, Blessed Padre Pio of Pietrelcina, and Mother Teresa of Calcutta.*

Do you want to be in their company?

WHY DOES OUR LORD ONLY CALL CERTAIN ONES?

As to why Christ calls only some, there is but one answer; namely, He calls them on account of a mysterious preference in His love.

Any other answer will miss the mark.

Why did Jesus prefer the twelve Apostles? Why did He love St. John above the others? Why did He have a special affection for Lazarus, Mary, and Martha?

The answer in each case is simply this: on account of a mysterious, affectionate preference.

When the young man in the gospel asked Our Lord what was the way to perfection, before replying *"Jesus, looking on him, loved him "* (Mk. 10: 21). Then He said, *"If you will be perfect, go sell what you have... and come follow Me"* (Mt. 19: 21).

Thus before He calls, Jesus looks lovingly upon the one He would call. This looking, this loving, remains a Mystery hidden in Jesus' Heart. Indeed, Jesus' choice of some persons was described precisely as *"a Mystery"* by Pope Paul VI. We do not and cannot know more.

Here we see a boy who is timid and frail. Jesus prefers him and chooses him from among many others. He is St. Dominic Savio.

Another lad burns with ardor and is not at all timid in his approach to Our Lord. Our Lord wants him, too, for His glory, and summons him to Himself. He is St. Gabriel of the Sorrowful Mother.

A girl who has been flighty, yet pure, ponders and dreams about her future. Jesus has a special love for her and picks her to be His spouse and a mother to many souls. She is St. Clare of Assisi.

Here is a mature man, experienced in the affairs and troubles of this world. Christ calls him to be a sailor on the bark of Peter, the Church and makes him a *"fisher of men"* (Mt. 14: 19). He is St. Ignatius of Loyola.

Again we find a laborer, a farmer, a student, a professional, who seem to be settled securely in their occupations. Jesus stops them, loves them, invites them, asks them, *"If you will be perfect..."* They are St. Felix of Cantalice, St. Camillus de Lellis, St. Francis Xavier, St. Alphonsus Liguori.

An energetic woman carries on much work within and outside her home. Jesus draws her to His Heart, discloses His Infinite Love to her, proposes a career of charity and self-sacrifice to her, in either a simple, contemplative life, or an active apostolic life. Such was a St. Jane Frances de Chantal, a St. Margaret Mary Alacoque, a St. Frances Xavier Cabrini.

Jesus has His own secrets about His love and they remain mysteries to us. But there is always His love and His love of preference or predilection, His exceptional love, His intimate love, and His full love— for creatures dear to Him.

Therefore when souls are called, their response ought to be ardent and generous, filled with boundless gratitude, in imitation of those Saints who, even in their advanced years used to kiss the walls of their religious house, blessing and thanking God for the sublime gift of a vocation.

On the day of her religious profession St. Margaret Mary Alacoque, in a transport of gratitude and of love for Him who had so highly favored her above others, wrote these words in her blood: *"Sister Margaret Mary, dead to the world. All is God's and nothing is mine. Let all be rendered to God and nothing to me. All is for His sake and nothing for mine."*

All those souls, great and little, who have tackled great obstacles and endured painful tribulations, so as not to lose so precious a treasure, must have understood, at least by intuition, the extraordinary value of this *"exceptional preferred status,"* as Vatican II calls the consecrated life.

Reflect on those brave girls — St. Clare of Assisi and St. Teresa of Avila — who were not afraid literally to run away from home so that they could enter religious life. St. Thomas Aquinas did the same, as well as the two lay brothers, St. Stanislaus Kostka and St. Gerard Majella. These beautiful, heroic examples are a witness to the power of Divine Love and the unconquerable zeal in virgins hearts.

No less beautiful are the cases of those who had to face economic difficulties and trials of different kinds in order to fulfill their vocation.

In the life of St. Pius X, we have edifying evidences of how he faithfully and courageously heeded the call of God.

At the age of twelve Joseph Sarto (his original name) asked his parents if he could study for the priesthood. The altar was the great attraction to him. He loved to serve Mass. The image of a priest celebrating the Holy Sacrifice charmed him and became an ideal of which he dreamed.

His parents were quite poor, but rich in the holy fear of God and in their trust in Divine Providence. They did not hesitate to seek a way for him to complete the studies that would prepare him for a seminary.

But how would they manage? They decided to send their boy to school at Castelfranco Veneto, a town seven kilometers from the Riese. After returning home in the evening, he would go to his parish priest for a Latin lesson.

And so every day for three years, rain or shine, the boy walked to and from school. In order not to wear out his shoes he would sling them across his shoulders, tied together with his lunch, as soon as he was out of town, and go barefoot.

At school, Joseph Sarto proved to be the best student. He won all the prizes. He was cheerful and charitable. His teachers regarded him with admiration.

Just reflect on the heroic spirit this boy showed in order to heed the call of Our Lord! Walking barefoot nine miles, rain or shine, for three years, carrying a meager meal. A remarkable boy!

Once he finally entered the seminary and a few years had passed, his father died, leaving a widow with eight children. It was a trying time. What was he to do? Should he return home and go to work to help his family? The decision was not to do so. Joseph and his mother entrusted themselves to Divine Providence. *"Entrust your way to the Lord and He will perfect your work"* (Ps. 36: 5). And so it was. Joseph continued in the seminary, making a brilliant record, earning the rank of *"outstanding."* Thus he continued, always a poor boy, always doing excellently.

No less were the problems that St. Maria Josephine Rossello had to surmount in order to correspond to the call of Our Lord.

"Maria Josephine, daughter of a craftsman of northern Italy, one day heard her father asking, 'Why are you always so serious?'

"Father, I would like to become a Sister," she answered.

Her father, who supported his family by making wicker ware, said, "Daughter, you know very well that you need a dowry like a girl getting married, and we are poor."

Maria resigned herself to her situation and became a maid in the home of an elderly married couple without children. They soon became so fond of her that they offered to will her their fortune, which was considerable, but under one condition, that she not become a Sister.

It was an appealing temptation, for she would be rich and be able to help her parents, especially her father, who continued at his craft in spite of his ill health.

Maria reflected at length on the attractive proposal, but in the end turned it down to pursue her long-cherished ideal. (Fr. Remo di Gesù, *Catechesis in Examples*, III, p. 1090.)

By refusing a rich earthly inheritance, the humble Maria Josephine consecrated herself to Jesus and became a great Saint and Foundress of a Congregation of Sisters.

Let us not forget that the parables of the Gospel which refer directly to the duty of corresponding to the grace of vocation are those of the *"Treasure hidden in the field"* (Mt. 13: 44), and of the *"Pearl of great price"* (Mt. 13: 45). In both parables the conduct of the finder of the treasure and the finder of the pearl is the same. Both sell all they have in order to have the treasure and the pearl.

A vocation is a treasure and a pearl of great price. One who receives a vocation knows what he must do according to Our Lord's word: he must sell all.

> *Are you, young reader, one of those whom Jesus is calling? Would you want to refuse this* "treasure," *this* "pearl of great price" *which is His call? Realize the responsibility you would have for this refusal. Consider well and listen to Our Lord within your heart. Perhaps He is looking upon you, loving you, and saying to you,* "If you will be perfect, go, and sell all... and then come follow Me" (Mk. 10: 21).

HOW DOES OUR LORD CALL?

Usually Jesus calls *"His close followers"* in the simplest, most natural way. He puts in a boy's or girl's heart a gentle, noble yearning, a sweet inclination, to pursue the things of God, to love Jesus, to imitate the Saints, to arrive at heroic holiness.

To become convinced of this it is enough to reflect on the childhood, for example, of St. John Bosco, St. Pius X, St. Maximilian Maria Kolbe, Blessed Padre Pio Pietrelcina — to mention those who are familiar. Consider also the girlhood of St. Bernadette, St. Thérèse of Lisieux, St. Gemma Galgani, St. Bertilla, Santina Campana.

We discover in these young hearts the presence and the activity of that golden thread of a vocation, which from then on developed ever more consistently, ever more beautifully.

But let us say at once that every human heart is a little world in itself, and that world is a mystery known only to God. In everyone there are features and characteristics that are unique and not found elsewhere. Nevertheless, the common way — in a sense the universal way — of perceiving Jesus' call lies in that attraction and spontaneous inclination towards sacred and Divine realities.

Then it will be the part of the spiritual director—always needed— to distinguish the presence of a real vocation and make sure of it, as well of its proper development through the soul's prompt and conscientious responding to grace. The pastor, the confessor, the spiritual director or counsellor has this heavy responsibility; for the task is given chiefly to these men to awaken and cultivate a vocation, to help it ripen, and to see that the soul cooperates with grace as promptly as possible.

We have been speaking especially of children. As for adolescents and adults, a vocation is evidenced by certain holy ambitions more analyzed and pondered. Thus, the desire to deliver our soul from the perils of worldly surroundings, to acquire holiness, to atone for our own sins and those of others, to imitate Jesus' life perfectly, to be an apostle in order to save souls— all these are supernatural ambitions and inspirations, one or another of which is sinking its roots in our heart and spurring us to renounce the world to give ourselves to Jesus and to become His close follower.

When St. Gerard Majella ran away from home, he was slipping out through a window when his mother cried, "What are you doing? Where are you going?" He cried back in a decisive tone, *"Mother, I'm going away to become a Saint!"*

St. Francis of Assisi left everything in order to imitate his poor, crucified Lord. St. Clare ran away from home to offer herself to a life of contemplative prayer and penance. St. Alphonsus left the career of an attorney-at-law in the Kingdom of Naples in order to dedicate himself to promote the saving truths of the Gospel among the most neglected poor. St. Frances Xavier Cabrini sacrificed everything in order to become the apostle to the poor immigrant class.

That is the way it has been. Every vocation has a secret wellspring of energy, which configures the life of the one called to Jesus and which enables one to imitate Our Lord in His virtues and deeds, thus being more and more absorbed by the dynamics of transforming love, until the soul can say with St. Paul, *"It is no longer I who live, but Christ lives in me"* (Gal. 2: 20).

At times Our Lord's summons comes unexpectedly, by chance— one could almost call it odd.

St. John of God, for example was nothing more or less than a wanderer. He had been a soldier, a herdsman, a peddler, a bookbinder. He wandered from place to place, from one occupation to another rather aimlessly. One day he entered a church and heard St. John of Avila preach. He listened attentively. The message deeply penetrated him. He entered into himself. Giving deep thought to his miserable condition, he firmly decided to give himself fully to God. So quick and decisive was the change that men took him to be demented.

Likewise Blessed Maria de Mattias, who founded the Sisters of the Precious Blood, hearing St. Gaspar of Bufalo preach, perceived Jesus' voice commanding her heart. She pledged herself at once to make a total gift of herself to God.

Picture St. Ignatius of Loyola, bedridden with an injured leg, wanting to read worldly novels according to his custom. But all he could find to read was a book recounting the life of Christ and some lives of the Saints. So he set about this reading just to relieve the boredom. He became radically changed.

The same happened to Brother Charles de Foucauld. By means of a spiritual book which suddenly enlightened his mind and heart, Our Lord shook him and called him.

In the chronicles of the Jesuit Order we read that St. Francis Borgia, Duke of Candia, gazing upon the decomposed body of Queen Isabel, then and there decided that he would quit the vanities of the world, resign from his high rank, and apply to become a Jesuit, as many other Spanish nobles were doing.

Here is an even more remarkable case. A father of a family was looking for a young tutor for his children. He found a student who favorably impressed him in spite of his poverty, which was such that he was scarcely making ends meet in his endeavor to continue in school. The gentleman took him into his home. He began to admire the young man's fine qualities. When the gentleman learned of his interest in the priesthood, he promised him every help. The youth hesitated to accept, because the offer seemed extravagant. However after consulting some qualified and prudent persons, he finally accepted and entered a seminary. He became the great St. Vincent de Paul.

The Servant of God Don Calabria was born of a poor Veronese Family. As a boy he found modest employment in a shop that made picture frames.

One day he accidentally soiled a diploma that he was framing. Making some angry remarks, the employer dismissed him. "Go and become a priest," he shouted, "for you are no good for anything else!" The poor boy, his eyes full of tears, answered, *"Very well, sir, I'll do just that!"*

Assisted by the charity of a poor priest, he managed with many sacrifices to get through a seminary and was ordained. Later on, he became the founder of the Poor Servants of Divine Providence. Pope Pius XII described him as a *"champion of evangelical charity."*

For some souls here or there the Lord's call may be something overwhelming, one might say violent, as it was with St. Paul. *"His voice was like the roar of many waters"* (Apoc. 1: 15).

In any case, for every chosen soul the Lord's summons is something personal, completely interior and secret. It is an operation of Divine Love. It is necessary that the heart be open and disposed to accept the gift. It requires humble and joyful gratitude. *"What shall I render to the Lord for all He has rendered me?"* (Ps. 115: 3). *"The Lord has done great things for us; He has filled us with joy"* (Ps. 125: 3). It demands generosity and promptness in responding to One who loves chosen souls as His favorites. *"Go before Him with exultation... Pass through His gates with hymns of thanksgiving; enter into His courts with songs of praise."* (Ps. 99: 2-4).

Young readers, give these matters thought. Perhaps Jesus has already let you feel an attraction for Him and His life of poverty, of virginity, of obedience. But perhaps you have let your liking for this world's goods snuff out this attraction, in order to satisfy the cravings of your body and the tendencies of your fallen nature toward earthly creatures. Open the eyes of your heart. Do not mistake values this way. It is fatal! Act in time lest "the Lord be angry and you perish from the just way" (Ps. 2: 12). *If, being summoned, you rightly respond, "you shall be a crown of glory in the hand of the Lord and a royal diadem in the hand of your God"* (Is. 62: 3).

Meantime you would do well to read St. Francis de Sales' *Treatise of the Love of God*, Book 8, chap. 10-14 to appreciate the virtues to practice and follies to avoid, in deciding about a state of life.

"Soon I will answer your call; soon I will belong wholly to You; soon I will have said good-bye to all that I love... it costs hardly anything when it is for You."

Photograph of Blessed Elizabeth of the Trinity, OCD before entering the convent.

WHEN SHOULD ONE RESPOND TO THE CALL OF JESUS?

It is necessary to respond *promptly* to Our Lord's call.

Twice in the holy Gospel a *prompt response* to Christ's call is reported. Once it was when Saints Peter and Andrew were called, and later when Saints James and John were called.

The Gospel tells us that Our Lord met the two brothers Peter and Andrew while they were casting their fishnets into the sea. He said, *"Follow Me, and I will make you fishers of men."* The two brothers did not delay a minute, but *"they immediately leaving their nets, followed Him"* (Mt. 4: 20).

Shortly afterwards Jesus met two other brothers who were fishermen, James and John. They were in a boat with their father mending their nets. Jesus also called them, and *"they forthwith left their nets and father and followed Him"* (Mt. 4: 22).

A *"prompt response"* is necessary when Jesus calls, leaving everything without delay, promptly separating even from what is near and dear— father, mother, home, occupation— to give oneself to Jesus. There cannot and should not be any other way of responding to the Divine summons.

St. Paul, thrown from his horse and blinded by a mysterious light, heard the Lord complain, *"Saul, Saul, why do you persecute Me?"* And he promptly responded, *"Lord, what will You have me to do?"* By this prompt cooperation and under Our Lord's guidance, he changed from a zealous, formidable persecutor, into a docile and meek follower, ready to do what Jesus asked and let himself be led where Our Lord directed.

What can be more beautiful than a call to belong entirely to Jesus, to be His minister or His spouse? Is this not perhaps the greatest honor that God gives a creature— one which many would like to have, but do not?

St. John Chrysostom advises, *"When Christ calls, He demands such prompt obedience from us that we must not delay even an instant."*

Any tarrying, any delay, can come only from the Enemy; and it can be fatal, as Jesus let that young man understand who, before becoming His follower, wanted to wait a little in order to say farewell first to his kindred. *"No man, putting his hand to the plow and looking back, is fit for the Kingdom of Heaven"* (Lk. 9: 62).

Later, when another young man asked to be able at least to go bury his father before following Jesus, Our Lord spoke the following stern words to him, *"Let the dead bury their dead"* (Lk. 9: 60).

One cannot dally with a vocation. It is an immense gift. It is offered, and can be withdrawn even at the first delay, with grave consequences for us, and causing great displeasure to Our Lord. Therefore St. Alphonsus dé Liguori says that, "when God calls someone to a more perfect state, he who does not want to put his eternal salvation in great danger must obey and obey *at once."* He says again, "Divine summons to a more perfect life are certainly special favors and very great ones, which God does not bestow upon everybody. Therefore, God very rightly becomes angry with whoever makes light of them."

What is the suitable age at which one should leave home? Considering the adjustments to be made, the ages of fifteen and sixteen are ideal for both boys and girls (17-18 in North America), provided they are counseled by a director who is spiritual and supernaturally wise. But it is better to act early than late. When a mother was about to accompany her fifteen-year-old boy to the Novitiate, a friend tried to counsel her, "Delay this a little, first let him know and enjoy a bit of the world."

"Ah! What kind of advice are you giving me?", the mother answered. "In that way I would be offering God spoiled fruit..."

It was a wise and holy answer. But— sad to say!— there are many who would foolishly say, when their innocent children are called by God, that they should first know the world, realize the evil in it, and then decide. This is pure foolishness.

Listen to this case found in the police court records of Anversa:

"A certain girl had always been good and devout. One day she informed her father of her wish to become a religious Sister. In order to steer her away from this idea, he gave her some obscene books. *'Read these first,'* he said, 'and then you will make your decision.'

"Not long afterwards the books had corrupted the girl, who became so bad that she killed her father... The court at Anversa condemned Mary Smolders, found guilty of patricide, to ten years of hard labor." (From *Via Verita Vita,* Sept. 1954, p. 429.)

What would you say if someone, when offered such a precious and rare gift whereby the Giver shows his special favor— what would you say if, instead of accepting it at once with joy, one reacted by delays and postponements that could compromise everything.

The Angelic Doctor St. Thomas Aquinas, who had to suffer a great deal in order to become a follower of Jesus, tells of the promptness we must show in answering Our Lord's call. He remarks that such calls bring us special lights which are not permanent, but fleeting. Therefore "the invitation to a more perfect life ought to be followed without delaying;" otherwise the Lord's voice passes away and He calls others.

When St. Francis of Assisi had a vision or dream at Spoleto, in which Our Lord asked him, why he ever left the Master to become a follower of the servant (to fight in battles near Apulia), the Saint answered like St. Paul, *"Lord, what would You have me to do?"* The Lord answered, "Return to the land that saw your birth."

St. Francis promptly obeyed. Then this so-called *"king of the young people of Assisi,"* whom few could equal in glamor and charisma, had to show no little courage to face the dishonor of returning to Assisi, almost like a deserter from military service, where no one could understand his being a quitter.

Now let us try to imagine what would ever have become of St. Francis if he had not promptly responded to Our Lord's bidding, but had gone on to Apulia?

If a Divine vocation is an extraordinary gift, it follows that one must by no means *"dilly-dally"* but he must act promptly in order not to risk losing so great a boon. One should not delay even a day, when he is to live in the house of the Divine Bridegroom.

The angelic St. Thérèse of Lisieux understood all this well when, because it would delay by a month her entrance into the convent of Carmel, she refused the gift of a trip to the Holy Land.

The courageous maidens St. Clare of Assisi and St. Teresa of Avila understood very well when they managed to run away from home so as not to delay consecrating themselves totally to Our Lord.

When St. Jane Frances de Chantal was a widow and her children were old enough and sufficiently well provided for, she decided to leave all in order to consecrate herself to God in the religious life under St. Francis de Sales' direction. Her son Celso Benigno, however, would not hear of it. To prevent his mother from leaving home he stretched himself out before the door. The sight moved the heroic mother to bitter tears. But presently she passed over her son to follow the voice of Our Lord.

One must be ready to make a courageous flight, a violent break with earthly ties— he must be ready to do all for Him who *"loved me and delivered Himself for me"* (Gal. 2: 20): for Him who now calls me among *"His own"*, so that I might be wholly, exclusively His, without *"divided"* heart (I Cor. 7: 33) totally consecrated to God's glory and the salvation of souls.

If I am convinced of all this, I will indeed make haste to answer the Lord's call, as the child Samuel did when he heard the Lord summon him from his sleep and he replied at once, *"Here I am!"* (I Kings 3: 5).

> *We say this to the young reader: Is there perhaps some bit of regret burning within you? If you are putting off from day to day the thought of seriously examining yourself about your true vocation, you perhaps realize that you are taking an unwise risk. Enter into yourself, listen, reflect, ponder the matter. Hasten to say, "Here I am Lord!" if you see that He calls you. Do not be hesitant and do not fear. Trust in the Lord as St. Paul did, who wrote,* "I can do all things in Him who strengthens me" (Phil. 4: 13). *What can seem hard to you now and perhaps make you delay, will by and by become easy as soon as you move on, as the Psalmist says,* "Blessed is the man whose help is from You... He shall advance from virtue to virtue" (Ps. 83: 6,8).

GOOD PARENTS AND PARENTS WHO ARE NOT SO GOOD

"When eleven-year-old Joseph Sarto, on his First Communion day, told his parents, *'I want to be a priest!'*, his mother smiled happily. But his father, John Baptist Sarto, had to support eight children on thirty lire a month, and he thought he could not afford the expense of a son in a seminary; so he was troubled.

"But when the pastor pointed out the boy's extraordinary aptitude for the priesthood, John bowed his head. Showing himself true to old Christian traditions, he answered with resignation and contentment, *'If God wants him, may He take him! He is His!'*" (Fr. Remo di Gesù, *Virtue in Examples,* I p. 848.)

Here we have the beautiful example of the holy mother and father of a Saint.

Alongside these parents of St. Pius X, we should remember the parents of St. John Bosco, St. Thérèse of Lisieux, St. Gemma Galgani, St. Maximilian Maria Kolbe, Blessed Louis Orione, Santina Campana, Blessed Padre Pio of Pietrelcina. These chosen children all came from sturdy homemakers, firm in the Faith, whose lives were exemplary.

Going back in time, we recall especially those holy mothers like St. Monica, who bore St. Augustine, St. Silvia, mother of St. Gregory the Great, Macrina, mother of St. Basil, and Antara, who was St. John Chrysostom's mother.

In the life of St. John Bosco we read this example of a wonderful Christian mother:

"On the eve of all Saints, 1851, Don Bosco had a preaching engagement in the parish of Castlenuovo d'Asti, his native town.

"The altar boy who escorted him to the pulpit attracted his attention. When they returned to the sacristy, he asked the boy what he intended to do with his life.

"'I want to go to Turin with you to become a priest.

"'*Fine! Let us hear what your mother has to say.*'

"After the mother had walked in, the Saint asked, '*Is it true, Teresa, that you have agreed to sell me your son?*'

"'Sell him? Oh, no! Our boys were given to us as gifts. They are not sold.'

"Don Bosco looked at the humble peasant woman, who revealed an uncommon greatness of soul. Then he replied in a tone of finality, '*I accept the gift!*'"

True Christian mothers not only give their children willingly to Our Lord, but they pray solicitously and earnestly that these children will be faithful to God's call. How many times has it been the mother who saved a child's vocation in a crucial moment?

Hear what happened to St. Maximilian Kolbe.

On the day before he was to take the religious habit, an unhappy idea from the devil persuaded him that he should go to the superior and announce that he would not take the habit of St. Francis. But just as he set out to see the Superior, his mother arrived to pay him a visit. The mother was quick to discover her boy's state of mind, and a few words were all she needed to change the boy's mind and bring him peace.

What shall we say of the mother of St. John Bosco? She literally would go without bread at times in order that her son might keep up his studies in the seminary. But she was glad to be poor, and was not backward about admonishing her son, "When you become a priest, if you have the great misfortune of getting rich, I will not even pay you a visit!"

There are deeply moving examples of parents who knew how joyfully to give their children to God and were solicitous about their vocation. By this they showed that they were not only parents physically, but spiritually as well, by spiritually forming them in piety and in Christian vision of life. At times such parents have known how to create in their homes an atmosphere stirring thoughts of Heaven rather than of earth.

For example, hear what St. Thérèse of Lisieux said of her family, which used to recite the Rosary every evening and listen to some words from their father and mother: *"Hearing our parents speak of eternity and holy things, we felt ourselves inclined to consider the things of the world as so many vanities, even though we were quite young..."*

A vocation is a golden seed. The Lord perhaps casts one or more in every Christian family. But what kind of soil is the family? Is it the soil along the roadside? Is it rocky soil? Is it soil choked with thorns? Or is it fertile and fruitful? (Lk. 8: 4-15) What a responsibility for every Christian family, especially for the parents!

A great boon for every truly Christian family is being numerous. A truly Christian couple knows how to accept all the children God sends them as God's gifts. They rightly shrink from every method or means that can frustrate a new creature's coming into the world either before or after its conception. In times past when vocations flourished, it was chiefly due to large families. Not only this, but how many Saints (also how many eminent artists and scientists) that we know of, would not have existed without large families? Here is a partial list of some Saints from large families:

Families of:

> Five children: St. Joan of Arc, St. Vincent de Paul, St. Margaret Alacoque.
>
> Six children: St. Charles Borromeo, St. Thomas Aquinas, St. John Vianney.
>
> Seven children: St. Bernard, St. Alphonsus Liguori.
>
> Eight children: St. Vincent Ferrer, St. Aloysius Gonzaga, St. Robert Bellarmine, St. Louis Grignon, St. Bernadette, St. Pius X, Blessed Padre Pio of Pietrelcina.
>
> Nine children: St. Therese of Lisieux, St. Raffaela of the Sacred Heart, Santina Campana
>
> Ten children: St. John Baptist de la Salle.
>
> Eleven children: St. Louis IX (King of France), St. Teresa of Avila, St. Catherine Laboure.
>
> Thirteen children: St. Ignatius of Loyola.

Fifteen children: St. Joseph Benedict Labre.
Sixteen children: St. Paul of the Cross.
Seventeen children: St. Francis Borgia.
Twenty-two children: St. Catherine of Sienna.

Large families are normal seedbeds for holy vocations. How is it that parents of today fail to understand this? Sad to say, we must admit that many parents who are thought to be Christian, can be outspoken against a society going bad and a corrupt world, whereas they themselves defile their marriage because they want no more than two or three children, and for years and years they sink to shameful bodily practices to prevent the arrival of new life— of God's gifts. If the question arises of giving one or two children to God, they react strongly against it. As for giving one of their two children to God— Never! Both are needed to serve the parents' selfish interests.

Pope Pius XII wisely declared, "We think we are not wrong to consider the disorder that is widely and radically upsetting marriage and the family as the cancer of modern society and the ruinous undoing of the work of salvation."

What would the same Pontiff say today when under civil law the family is legally permitted to use contraceptives, abortion, end itself by divorce. Everywhere today examples are easy to find where bestiality is introduced into families (by contraception), assassination (by abortion), and auto-destruction (by divorce). And all this with the aid and protection of the civil authority.

Such are the distressing facts!

And we are not finished. We must speak of all those parents who, instead of accepting the vocation of a child — once they have sufficiently discovered it — hinder it and use every means to fight it.

In this regard let us say here with the great masters of the spiritual life (conspicuous among them St. Thomas Aquinas and St. Alphonsus Liguori), that if one's parents are not persons of fully proven faith (like those of St. Thérèse of Lisieux and St. Pius, for example), they are not the right counselors about a Divine vocation, but almost always are rather its first enemies. And what of parents who would foolishly high-pressure a son to become a priest or a daughter to become a Sister, whether they have the vocation or not? These parents, though rarely found, are enemies also of the Divine Will calling each one to this or that vocation or state in life.

The ties of flesh and blood easily bring an unreasoning blindness to the minds and hearts of family members, rendering them ready to swear again and again that there is certainly no true vocation, but that the son (or daughter) has been unduly swayed by this or that priest (or sister). Instead of reasoning, they talk foolishness. They speak only according to emotions, not according to Faith like true Christians.

Sometimes, after having tried to gain his parents' consent and having found them unjustly hostile and inflexible against a true vocation, matters reach the point when a sufficiently adult son or daughter can no longer obey them in this regard. It then becomes lawful, even a duty, for a child to leave his parents, even by running away from home, as, for example, St. Francis and St. Clare did, as well as St. Teresa of Avila and St. Gerard Majella.

"We must obey God rather than men" (Acts 5: 29). It is obvious. And if the pain of leaving one's family grows fiercer during the struggle and during the flight, Christ foresaw this when He said, *"I have come not to bring peace, but the sword. For I have come to divide son from father..."* (Mt. 10: 34).

One can scarcely forget the awesome, painful rift between St. Francis of Assisi and his father. Unhappy father! Disappointed in his worldly ambitions for his son, he raged against him, disowning him and disinheriting him. And Francis, left penniless and half-naked, was able to fervently raise his voice and sigh, *"Now I can truly say, 'Our Father who art in Heaven!'"*

St. Alphonsus de Liguori confessed that the most painful trial of his life was when he told his father his decision to leave the world to consecrate himself to God. As soon as his father realized his decision, he grabbed hold of him and, weeping, clung to him for three hours saying, *"O my son, do not abandon me! O son, my son! I do not deserve this treatment!"*

But St. Alphonsus, his heart no less grieved, remained constant and firm to the end, reflecting on Our Lord's Divine words, *"He that loves father or mother more than Me, is not worthy of Me"* (Mt. 10: 37).

Likewise St. Teresa of Avila, a girl remarkable for her goodness and talent, did all she could to convince her good father that she should leave home and enter the convent. But he kept declining, feeling unable to give up that lovable, firstborn daughter who was a comfort and support for his large family. Finally Teresa had to run away from home. She suffered so that when she reached the gate of the convent she felt as though all her bones were shaken out of place. After that, her father's distress changed into peace and joy.

Let parents guard against standing in the way of their children's vocations! We repeat St. Gregory Nazianzen's caution: *"Once a person has picked the wrong vocation, his whole life is in error and all goes wrong."* When someone stands in the way to his son's or daughter's vocation, he moves him or her to take the wrong path, to become unsuccessful and out of place— a misfit. The will of God is not something with which we should play. And any and every punishment is possible sooner or later for the parents of any who do not cooperate.

This impressive account from the life of St. John Bosco is a lesson for all parents:

"One day Don Bosco went to visit Countess D. L. and her four sons. When, at her request, he had blessed them, she said, 'Tell me, Don Bosco, what will my sons be?'

"*'God alone knows the future!'*", was the reply.

"'I realize that,' the lady said, 'but tell me something— at least the way you would forecast it.'

"Then the Saint, in a jesting way, took them one by one.

'This one will be a general. This next one will become a great statesmen. Henry will be a famous physician.'

"Delighted at these forecasts, the countess turned to her fourth son.

"'We will make a very fine priest out of him,' said St. John Bosco.

"These words greatly upset the mother, who was strongly prejudiced against a priestly vocation.

"'Never! Him a priest? I would rather see him dead!"

Don Bosco then departed very coldly.

A few months later Don Bosco received an urgent call to go to the lady's home, because her little boy was gravely ill. The Saint was very reluctant to go, but went simply because of her repeated insistence.

The child, now despaired of by the physicians, reminded his mother of the words she had spoken during Don Bosco's previous visit, and the Saint then confirmed them, saying, "*Your words, Countess, were confirmed definitively by God when you pronounced them!*"

The Divine decree could not be revoked.

Young reader, think seriously of your responsibility. Give an ear to your Lord within your heart. If He makes you hear Him calling you to consecrate yourself, do not be overcome by dread or fear of obstacles that might come from your parents to your vocation. Remember St. Francis and St. Clare and the heroic, victorious flight they took in order to find and follow Our Lord. Have courage, and if it is necessary, do not hesitate to imitate them. When the Lord calls souls, He knows how to make them into eagles who soar up to Heaven.

Photograph of Ven. Fr. Damien de Veuster, a 33 year old priest of the Fathers of the Sacred Hearts of Jesus and Mary, when he volunteered to work with the lepers at Molokai.

PRAYER AND VOCATIONS

"Pray to the Lord of the harvest, that He send laborers into His harvest." (Mt. 9: 38).

From our Divine Lord's word it appears obvious that the gift of vocations is linked to prayer and is the fruit of prayer.

One can say without hesitation that prayer is the mother of vocations. Every other means, every other device, all other resourcefulness and effort to obtain vocations, are not enough, nor can they ever replace prayer, the true mother of every vocation.

Pius XI once admonished religious superiors:

"It is not our task to look for numbers, since it is not given to us to inspire a vocation in souls... It comes from God and only God can give it. It is our task to nurture this vocation, to enrich it, and to adorn it." (Address of Sept. 14, 1932).

One can also say without hesitation that where one finds vocations, they are a sign that there has been prayer; whereas where there are no vocations, it is a sign that prayer is lacking or there is not enough of it.

Among those families, those seminaries, those convents, monasteries, Orders, and Congregations where there are no vocations or vocations are rare, it is a sign that prayer has yielded its place to action and the result is simply time wasted. It is a sign that, instead of praying, people prefer to fight by so-called vocational activities— projects, workshops, centers, studies, research, *"experiences."*

How naive this is! Do we know better than Jesus? If He has urged us simply to pray to obtain vocations, is it not evident that prayer is the substantial means, while all the rest is just marginal?

St. Maximilian Maria Kolbe declared, *"Active work is good, but compared to prayer it is secondary and even less than secondary."* And he proved that prayer comes first in bearing fruit, by building two *Cities of the Immaculate* peopled with two powerful armies of friars.

Giving first place to prayer— intense, lengthy, patient prayer— other means can also be used to aid the cause of vocations. But without prayer, or with prayer notably curtailed, all the other means will prove a complete failure.

It is something noteworthy on this subject that Blessed Fr. Hannibal de Francia founded the Institute *"Rogate"*, taking its name from the *Latin* of Our Lord's words *"Pray to the Lord of the harvest."* And the flourishing of vocations which followed directly depended on the many, many prayers being said.

Do you want more examples of the fruitfulness of prayer in winning vocations?

Let us ask ourselves, why did the great Patriarchs and religious Founders— St. Benedict and St. Bernard, St. Francis and St. Clare, St. Dominic and St. Ignatius, St. Teresa and St. Alphonsus— why did they have so many vocations? Why does Mother Teresa of Calcutta have so many vocations today? How have they come about?

There is just one answer. They first got on their knees with their companions to pray. They prayed at length, hour after hour every day of their lives.

"The most important hours for my communities," says Mother Teresa of Calcutta, *"are the four hours of community prayer each day."* And vocations are the fruit.

Let us ask ourselves again: How have many Christian families managed to furnish one and even more vocations for the Church?

The answer if still the same: Numerous prayers beget vocations.

At the beginning of the last century a certain lady spent an hour a day in adoration before the Blessed Sacrament to obtain the favor that at least one of the children whom she would bear— and she bore ten— might consecrate himself to God.

Year after year she persevered in her daily hour of adoration. Of her ten children, nine consecrated themselves to Our Lord, and one of these became the celebrated Cardinal Nicholas Patrick Wiseman, author of the beautiful book *Fabiola*.

Another lady, also English, for twenty years likewise made an hour of adoration daily before the Blessed Sacrament, asking that, if it be God's will, He grant that her sons and daughters be consecrated to Him. She knew that every vocation is a kind of miracle, and so she persevered courageously in this daily prayer.

What was the fruit? Her five daughters became Sisters of Charity. Six of her sons became priests, of whom two were Bishops and one was Cardinal Herbert Vaughan, Archbishop of Westminster, much respected also by Anglicans.

Her Cardinal son, speaking of his mother, revealed that she was a model of virtue, devoted in particular to the Sacred Heart, to the Holy Eucharist, and to Our Lady. He recalled how he had seen her spend hours on her knees before the Blessed Sacrament, and this example deeply edified the whole family.

Furthermore, who can say how many vocations which have blossomed forth here and there, even where nothing seemed to favor them, have been due to many unobtrusive, unknown prayers. Such is the power of prayer, which works in unseen ways wherever God wills!

L'Osservatore Romano of May 29, 1929, contains the following striking testimony concerning the Bishop of Mainz:

"Once when he was celebrating Mass in a convent, Msgr. Ketteler, Bishop of Mainz (1811-1887) was greatly moved at the sight of a Sister as he distributed Holy Communion. Those same features he had seen before, but under different circumstances.

"After the Mass he expressed a desire to speak to the Community. When the Sisters were assembled, the Bishop did not see the one who had so moved him. He asked whether everybody was present, and learned that an elderly Sister was missing who had chores in the kitchen and wanted to be dispensed from this assembly.

"She was summoned, and appeared before him when the others had left. A question was put to her: How had she been able to make herself still useful to souls?

She answered that she was completely absorbed in her work in the kitchen, but that she offered God her actions and sufferings. One hour would be for the Pope, one for the Bishop, one for the missions, and at night she dedicated an hour for *the conversion of those young intellectuals called to the priesthood but who were neglecting their vocation.*

"Deeply impressed, the Bishop urged the Sister to continue her worthy apostolate, and he dismissed her with his blessing.

"Later he told the Superiors, *'It is to that Sister that I owe my own conversion from a frivolous life. One night when I was absorbed in having a good time at a ball, I suddenly saw a face before me which gazed on me with intense pity. I was bewildered. I then gave some thought to the strange apparition, understood the vanity of my conduct, changed my life, and entered the seminary.'*

"'*This morning when I was distributing holy Communion I was surprised to recognize the same face that appeared to me that night, precisely at the time when she prays for frivolous young men who are neglecting their vocation. Let her remain unaware of the great good she did for me. She has no need of encouragement in order to continue her fruitful apostolate.'*"

How important it is to pray for vocations, even if we do not know whom our prayers will help!

Someone may ask: Can someone who has no vocation pray to obtain a vocation for himself?

Certainly. As for a vocation to the priesthood, one ought to pray with the condition, *"If it be God's will."* But be sure the vocation to become a Saint is something God wants us to pray for, and will grant if we keep praying and cooperating with the graces he metes out to us. Moreover, if the vocation is a special gift, God can grant it any time and at any age. Just reflect on all those souls who began to follow Christ as mature adults.

One should think particularly of all those young people — even mature ones — who have never come to a decision, saying they cannot learn with certainty what way to take, what state to embrace. Should they marry? Or seek the priesthood? Or be a monk? Or a friar? A religious Sister? Or a contemplative? Or a missionary? Oh, the confusion and the suffering! When our mind goes around in circles, what are we to do?

One needs to escape the dilemma as soon as possible. Otherwise he is in serious danger of *spending his life* running around in circles. How to get out of this plight?

Let us hear the suggestion of a great master of vocational problems, St. Alphonsus Liguori. In an open letter which he published, he advised an unnamed person to make a retreat of eight or ten days of intense prayer in a secluded spot, like a monastery or friary. During this time of recollection and meditation, the Saint would have him offer up fervent appeals to Our Lord and Our Lady. "*Conduct me, O Lord, in Your way, and I will walk in Your truth*" (Ps. 85:11). "*Make the way known to me, wherein I should walk... Teach me to do Your Will*" (Ps. 142: 8,10).

The holy Doctor tells his correspondent to take with him to the place of seclusion "*a book of meditations to read in place of hearing conferences.*" He should make his meditation "*in the morning and in the evening, with a half hour of reflection each time.*" He should also take with him some *"lives of the Saints or another spiritual book for reading. These will be your only companions in the solitude of the eight days."*

In order for the retreatant to receive *"light and hear what the Lord says,"* he must *"stay far away from distractions."* To perceive *"the Divine calls one must break off dealing with the world. No remedies help the sick man if he does not take due care of himself, as by avoiding harmful exposure and harmful food."* Likewise, *"So that the exercises may assist you in the salvation of your soul you need to avoid harmful distractions, such as receiving visits from friends, or messages ... or letters."* Alphonsus advises him to *"lay aside letters"* and not read them *"until the exercises are finished."* He instructs him to avoid *"reading curious books or doing any studies."* He should rather *"study only the crucifix."* In his room he should have no book *"except what is spiritual"* and when he reads them he should not do so *"out of curiosity, but only for reaching"* the goal of his retreat — in this case, the determination of his state of life.

The avoidance of external distractions is *"not enough,"* St. Alphonsus says. *"One needs to remove internal ones"* too. If one *"deliberately turns his thoughts to things of the world or to his studies or the like, the exercises and the solitude will be of little value."* While one makes the exercises he *"needs to use the time only for the interests of the soul, without wasting a moment."*

In order to make a fruitful retreat, receiving the lights and graces needed for wise resolutions and decisions about one's problems, what dispositions must one take with him? It should be holy indifference, that disinterested, unbiased attitude that merely wants to decide everything according to God and to please Him alone. While St. Alphonsus prescribes this disposition for his correspondent to start his retreat, we presume, judging from the retreat matter he composed, that he considers retreatants must at least go on retreat with the desire to use this true, disinterested wisdom, and the retreat reflections should help one cultivate it. In any case, the decisions and resolves reached in the course of the retreat should be made with this indifference. Otherwise, *"instead of conforming to God's Will,"* it would be a matter of wanting *"God to conform"* to our will. One would be *"like a pilot who pretends to want his vessel to move, but he does not truly want this, who casts anchor and then hoists the sails. The Lord does not enlighten or speak to such a person. But if you beg God with indifference and a willingness to fulfill His Will, He will let you know clearly the best state of life for you."*

At the end of these days of prayer, let one reach his resolution at God's inspiration, such as it may be, in the way the holy Doctor counsels, and let him keep to it as a fruit of prayer. The Lord does not allow us to be deceived by such prayer.

St. Augustine tells us: *"If you are not called, act in such wise that you may be called"* — may be called, that is, to total generosity with God. Such is the way things will work. Lengthy, persevering prayer can obtain this grace, and the light and inspiration to know the form of generosity to which God would call us. Sometimes persistent prayer obtains this in surprising ways, as happened to a young American, as told in *L'Osservatore Romano* of July 31, 1954: "A young American in his twenties had been an army captain, had graduated from Fordham University's School of Commerce, and had held a good position with General Motors, which paid him a high salary. He decided to make a brief spiritual retreat with the Trappists.

"The first day he said to his companion, *'This is certainly not the place for me.'*

"The second day he remarked, 'Well, after all, it is not altogether bad.'

"The third day, 'I must go to see the Abbot.'

"On the fourth day he came to see me (writes the Abbot). I explained life in the monastery and made this remark, 'My dear Henry, for your night's sleep I can offer you only a straw mattress stretched over two planks of wood. We go to bed at 7 P.M. and rise at midnight. Sundays we rise earlier in order to chant all the responsaries for the Readings at Matins.

"As choir monks we spend from six to seven hours a day in church for our chanted office and the conventual Mass...

"There is also time dedicated to spiritual reading and private prayer. Even if you become a priest, you will have to do manual labor in the fields or shop, like the Divine Workman of Nazareth. In other words, you will have to make a complete sacrifice of yourself to Jesus.

"And — I concluded — you see, Henry, it is not a case for giving 95 percent, or even 99.50 percent, but a hundred percent.

"Henry answered, *'I want to give myself a hundred percent. I want to give everything. This thought is like a fire in my soul. I will come back in six months."*

"He came back after three months."

We must add that prayer is necessary, is indispensable, for another reason: to preserve a vocation until death. " *Hold firmly what you have, that no man take your crown*" (Apoc. 3:11). Now from whom will this firmness come if not from Our Lord? *"I have kept the ways of the Law,"* prays the Psalmist, *"that my footsteps be not moved"* (Ps. 16: 4-5).

We can say of many people who were once consecrated to God, that if they had remained faithful to the practice of praying at length each day, they would never have betrayed their Lord.

Love feeds on love. Personal love feeds on personal love. A vocation is personal love on the part of Jesus. Prayer is the meeting, the interchange of personal love with Jesus on the part of a soul. If this interchange, this meeting, is lacking, love dwindles and ceases, and the vocation cannot survive.

For this reason one can rightly declare that St. Alphonsus Liguori's celebrated maxim, *"He who prays, is saved; he who prays not, is lost,"* applies to consecrated souls in particular way. For them it can mean, *"He who prays, saves his vocation; he who prays not, loses it."*

With prayer a vocation is not only safeguarded, but it becomes ever more firmly established, as St. Peter desires it to be when he bids us to *"make sure your calling and election"* (II Pet. 1:10).

We ask the young reader to reflect earnestly. Why not make a test? Perhaps you have never done it. Apply yourself to intense prayer. See if you can perhaps find a desirable place, and give yourself over to an experience of exceptionally earnest prayer, asking light from Him to see your way clearly. Bear in mind that we must turn in prayer to Our Lord that "He will teach us His ways" and that "we will walk in His paths" (Is. 2:3). *Jesus alone is the Way to the Kingdom of Heaven.* "Come you to Him and be enlightened" (Ps. 33: 6). *In prayer you will be enabled to see your soul acquire that radiant peace of* "those souls chosen by the Lord," *who is not indifferent to our choices, especially regarding a vocation.*

"Lord of this house, do You accept me?"

Photograph of Servant of God Sr. Faustina Kowalska.

"I was born poor, I have lived in poverty and I shall end my days a poor man."

Photograph of Pope St. Pius X,
when he was the Bishop of Mantua.

THE CALL TO HOLINESS—
DANGERS OF THE WORLD

Do you realize that out of a hundred canonized Saints, *seventy* are religious, *twenty* are Popes, Bishops, and priests, *five or six* are laypersons who lived single, consecrated lives in the world, and *three or four* are married persons?

The real seedbeds of Saints on earth, then, are religious houses.

Reflect well: Seventy percent of the Saints come from that group who have religious vocations, who hear Jesus' call, *"Go sell all... Come, follow Me"* (Mk. 10:21).

It is not hard to reach the conclusion, then, that one who "follows Jesus," quitting the world, becomes a Saint more easily than if he stayed in the world as a layman or married person. Blessed Padre Pio of Pietrelcina wisely remarked that "in the world people recollect themselves but little and think things through but little."

With this, let it be clear we do not deny the possibility of becoming a Saint in the world as a single layperson or as a married person. It is enough to think of the many Saints who were laymen and married. To mention a few, we may recall St. Louis IX, King of France, St. Elizabeth, Queen of Hungary, Blessed Columbini, Blessed Anna

Maria Taigi— shining examples of husbands and wives, of fathers and mothers of families.

But it remains true that the difficulties in becoming a Saint in the world are greater and heavier, if we consider that out of a hundred Saints, only three or four were married. Agreed precisely, because it is not impossible, all married Christians can and should reach holiness. But unfortunately the greater part are shipwrecked as regards holiness, even though some attain a high degree of holiness, and, we must add, all can at least save themselves from going to hell.

In any case, the plight of Christians in the world calls for reflection on the question of vocation and on what path one is to take. It is a very serious matter and deserves to be taken to heart as a grave matter of conscience, if we reflect that no Christian is free to decide as he pleases whether to seek holiness or not; for it is the strict duty of all.

I said that the pursuit of holiness is the *duty of all*. It is certainly God's Will for everybody, as St. Paul clearly says: *"This is the Will of God, your sanctification"* (I Thes. 4: 3). No one is excluded from this noblest of duties. It would be shamefully childish to shun it on the grounds that one is not a priest, or friar or sister— as though only consecrated souls had the obligation to seek personal holiness.

The point we emphasize here is just this: I may be only a simple Christian living in the world. I even may be married. I may even be involved in the affairs of the world and have no calling to be one of those consecrated to God. But I have the same duty they have to become a Saint; for *"This is the Will of God, your sanctification"* (I Thes., 4: 3).

This doctrine is clearly confirmed by Vatican II in a full chapter of the Constitution on the Church.

This is a subject on which one might become very discouraged, considering the tragic condition of the world. The mere mention of striving for holiness in the world seems almost folly, since some consider it a miracle if a person manages to keep his soul even free from mortal sin while living in the world! Considering the world as it is— with its scandals, seductions, deceptions— the real stimulus that moves men to avoid its wickedness is not the desire to achieve holiness, but the desire to escape damnation.

All this is the unfortunate truth. Hereby we understand why the young St. Bernard, frightened of the dangers of the world, turned away from his family's riches and withdrew to the Abbey of Citeaux, and by his example and words drew after him five of his brothers, an uncle, thirty other kinsmen and friends, and even his seventy-year-old father.

Now perhaps one can better appreciate the reaction of the famous "King of Verse," William Divini, celebrated poet of Campidoglio, when he chanced to see St. Francis of Assisi and hear him preach on the folly and vanity of the world. After the sermon he cast himself at the Saint's feet and begged him, "O Brother Francis, take me far away from men and consecrate me to God. Take away these worldly clothes and clothe me in the garment of paradise!" St. Francis soon let him put on the serge habit of his friars and girded him with the cord. He called him "Brother Pacifico"— meaning peace— *because the Saint at last had enabled him to find true peace of heart.*

By considering *"the world with its concupiscence"* (I Jn. 2: 17), one can better appreciate the great value of a worthy religious and priestly vocation, of the consecration to God which should be a great encouragement and spur to fulfill the duty all of us have to achieve personal holiness.

To use a comparison of St. Joseph Cafasso, an unworldly priest's life, and even more so that of a holy religious who has forsaken the world, is like a gentle-flowing stream whose waters stay limpid and pure and within its banks; whereas life in the world is like a turbulent river which, with the melting snow, turns into rapids, overflowing its banks, while its waters, once limpid, become slimy billows that flood the countryside, damaging and destroying crops and homes.

In the life of St. Francis Xavier Cabrini we read that one day the Saint was reflecting on a tragic fact that the *"whole world is under the wicked one"* (the devil) (I Jn. 5: 19). She then considered the gift of a religious vocation to be so precious that she set out to take the greatest care to preserve all such vocations, even those that could be considered mediocre and of inferior quality, requiring great patience for their formation. The Saint even ventured to induce other communities of Sisters to send her their novices whom they would not accept for profession. Nearly always the Saint managed to form them herself and bring them to great perfection.

At this point we need to address especially those youths, those men and women, who are hesitating about how to respond to Our Lord, or are unsure about their holy vocation, and are reaching the conclusion, perhaps too easily and superficially, that "After all is said and done, one can be a good father of a family in the world, or a good mother."

Yes, one can. But for the sake of God and your soul, we ask you to give us your attention. First of all, if one is called to the married life, one needs not just to become a "*good father*" or a "*good mother*", but the vocation is to be a "*holy father*" and a "*holy mother*". Personal holiness is something more than simple goodness. Furthermore, *one can* be a "holy father" and a "holy mother" if one is called to the married life. But if married life is not the path indicated by God, then by choosing that state one takes the wrong course, and it will then be much harder for him to manage to be even a "good father" or a "good mother". Yes, it is naive to take refuge in the thought that "*one can*" become holy in the world, when we know that married Saints nowadays are, sad to say, few.

Here is something written by St. Alphonsus with his customary wisdom: "Commonly men of the world make no scruple over telling poor young people who are called to the religious state that one can serve God everywhere, and therefore in the world also. And the strange thing is that such statements sometimes come from the lips of priests, and even of religious— but of those religious who either became religious without a vocation or who do not know what a vocation is. Yes, it is true that one who is not called to the religious life can serve God... elsewhere, but not one who is called to the religious life and who chooses capriciously to remain in the world. It will be hard for him to live an upright life and serve God." (*Works on the Religious State*, Op. 1, n. 2, v. i.)

Whoever is tempted to waver or to linger long in uncertainty over his vocation, should consider well the risk of losing *"the treasure hidden in a field"* (Mt. 13:44), the one *"pearl of great price"* (Mt. 13: 46) — goods of priceless value spoken of in the Gospel, which set the favored creature on the royal road to holiness.

You, O young reader, are you, too, perhaps among the number of those who are hesitating, undecided about their vocation? Are the world and creatures luring you? It may be true that you have no intention of using them sinfully — neither the world nor creatures. Yet you know very well that in the world and amid creature comforts it will be easier for you to damn yourself than to grow in holiness. Why take the risk? Overcome your uncertainty by gazing upward. God wants you to be holy like Jesus.

ACTIVE AND CONTEMPLATIVE VOCATIONS

"I want to give myself entirely to God. In what ways can I do this?"

It almost seems like an unnecessary question, but it is not. It is not enough that you be ready to consecrate yourself to God in any way chosen at random. One who is to give himself to God must do so in the way God wants. In every holy vocation one can distinguish different characteristics. At the very least it is dangerous to pay no heed to them. If God wants me to be consecrated to Him in the active apostolate, I would do wrong to give myself to Him in a Trappist monastery. If He wants me in a Trappist community, I do wrong to dedicate myself to Him in an active, less sheltered community, or in the world.

Let us roughly outline the possible ways one can dedicate himself to God.

1. The first way — wholly interior — is the *private vow of virginity or of chastity*, of one who remains a layperson in the world, having his own domestic or professional tasks. Instances of such dedication were St. Gemma Galgani and St. Joseph Moscati.

2. A more stable way is to belong to a Secular Institute of perfection for men or for women, in which the three vows of *obedience, poverty, and chastity* are taken. These dedicated souls live with their own families, supporting themselves in some employment at home or outside the home. Among such institutes approved by the Church, there is, for example the *S.A.C.R.I. Association.*

3. A sacramental consecration is that of the diocesan *priest* who lives with his close kin or alone in his parish (perhaps with another priest), under the law of celibacy and obedience to his bishop. He serves as a minister of God and dispenser of the Divine mysteries.

4. The fourth kind of dedication is that of *religious* in the mixed life, that is, whose life is both contemplative and active, and is lived according to the three vows in religious communities, in monasteries, convents, priories, religious houses, sometimes combined with missionary life.

5. The fifth form of dedication is that of the *monk* or *nun* in a purely (or predominantly) contemplative life, lived in monasteries and strictly cloistered convents. The three vows are taken, and the community life is more austere and strenuous. These have included especially the Trappists of the Strict Observance, the Camaldolese hermits, and the Carthusians. The strictly *eremitical life* is classed as purely contemplative.

What we have said should serve as a sufficient sketch, along general lines, of the different forms of consecrated life.

When we descend to particulars, however, it must be admitted that apart from the consecrated life in the world (lay institutes and private vow) and that of the diocesan priest— which appear simpler and clearer in their form and structure— vocational orientation and choice become more difficult in regard to two forms of this life: *active-contemplative* (religious life) and a life *solely contemplative* (monastic life).

The orders and congregations are so many! To mention just few: Benedictines, Franciscans, Dominicans, Carmelites, Servites, Jesuits, Christian Brothers, Camillians, Passionists, Salesians... The better part of which have female branches. Countless are the communities strictly for women, beginning with such holy founders as St. Vincent de Paul and subsequent foundations. More recent are the religious families (of men or women or of both) which have been inspired by Charles de Foucauld and those founded by Don Alberione, Blessed Orione, Blessed Guanella, Mother Speranza and Mother Teresa of Calcutta.

Examples of purely contemplative, monastic orders are many: for men, Benedictines, Trappists, Carthusians and Camaldolese (hermits); and for women, Benedictine nuns, Poor Clares, Carmelites, Visitandine nuns, Passionist nuns.

It goes without saying that this flowering not only is not a problem, but enriches consecrated life in the Church. There is a place for everyone and for every aspiration!

One who feels drawn to the Evangelical life of St. Francis of Assisi, of St. Anthony of Padua, of St. Paschal Baylon, of St. Maximilian Maria Kolbe, should join the Franciscans.

One who experience pity for the sick, the suffering and needy, should apply to the sons of St. Camillus de' Lellis or of St. John of God or of Bl. Guanella.

One who feels attracted to serve the young and children should enter the Salesians or Christian Brothers, great educators of the young.

One who seeks the wonderful transport of the spirit in silence, in solitude, in hiding, should apply to a Trappist or Carthusian monastery.

One who desires a form of religious life more engaged in study, and in battling for the Church should consider the Dominican and Jesuits.

One who aspires to do missionary work can apply where opportunities are offered to go to mission lands.

Girls who have been charmed by the religious life of St. Bertilla and Blessed Augustina Pietrantoni, holy virgins full of charity for the sick, should consider some Congregation that calls for generous service to the sick.

Young people preferring to dedicate themselves to the education of children and youth, may look into some Congregation devoted to this work.

Those who would share the plight of the poorest of the poor in order to assist and relieve them, may consider the Little Sisters of Jesus and especially the Missionary Sisters of Charity of Mother Teresa of Calcutta.

Girls feeling a powerful attraction to sacrifice themselves entirely as a holocaust in the *"hidden life with Christ in God"* (Col. 3:3), as in the life of St. Clare, St. Veronica, St. Thérèse of Lisieux, may consider one of those monasteries with total enclosure. (Poor Clares, Carmelites).

But here is something that should be urged upon everyone interested in a consecrated life: He should not enter a community where there is no assurance that the life offered is one perfectly faithful to the Founders and to the Rules by which the Order has produced Saints. Today more than ever this is a painful point to make; but we are all the more obliged to make it. It is folly to enter where the life is unfaithful to the ideals, unobservant, and in a state of relaxation that destroys the very substance of a program pledged by its nature to sacrifice and daily immolation. It is better to look elsewhere, says St. Alphonsus— better not to enter. The Lord will preserve the grace of His call in the upright and faithful hearts that duly desire to find a faithful and grace-laden religious family.

God certainly does not call all to the same vocation, nor to the consecrated life in an Order or Institute; for *"every one has his proper gift from God: one after this manner, and another after that"* (I Cor. 7:7). But the importance of putting God first in charity is paramount.

"I am not against those who gave thought to temporal suitabilities when they enter their state of life and seek employment; but I am sure that a failure to turn first to God, making Him the single, final goal of all our considerations, and the failure to carefully consider whether a particular state, a particular prospective spouse, or a particular career or position, is the one better suited for our salvation— this failure is a disorder of disastrous consequences."

According to the doctrine of St. Anthony Claret *(Mission Sermon, 3: 285 f. 1858 ed.)* when one's motives are perfectly upright, he is apt to consult wisely and decide wisely, and if his vocation is for the consecrated life, he is apt to check and see to it that the community he enters is one that is faithful to the ideals of the Holy Founders and that it appeals principally to supernatural motivation. A vocation to the consecrated life is something the majority of people do not have, and it is something very precious, being a sign of God's special favor.

St. Alphonsus Liguori writes:

"One who feels he is called by God to enter an observant religious institute should understand that the plan of any observant community is to follow as closely as possible in the footsteps and example of the Holy Life of Jesus Christ, which was one of total detachment and mortification, full of suffering and contempt. I said *'observant institute',* for if it is not observant it would be better to remain in the world than to enter a community where the observance is relaxed" — whether as to discipline or as to doctrine we say.

"Therefore," he continues, *"one who is resolved to come to an observant community should at the same time resolve to come to suffer and deny himself in everything, according to what Jesus Himself said to those who would give themselves over to following Him perfectly: ' If anyone would come after Me, let him deny himself and take up his cross and follow Me'* (Mt. 16: 24)."

Furthermore he adds:

"Let one who wishes to enter the religious life not forget to resolve to become a Saint and to undergo every exterior and interior suffering in order to be faithful to God and not forsake his vocation. And if he is not resolved upon this, I urge him not

to deceive the superior and himself and not to embrace that life. For this reluctance is a sign that he is not called, or— which would be worse— that he is not choosing to correspond to the vocation as he should." (Works on the Religious State., I, v. f.)

Without limiting the total generosity with Divine Wisdom which everyone is called upon to strive for and by grace attain, St. Francis de Sales has this to say about the various counsels, the heroic ways, people may feel called to practice generosity:

"The Savior says, *'If you will be perfect, go, sell what you have, and give to the poor, and follow Me'* (Mt. 19: 21; Lk. 18: 22). Now the loving heart receives... the counsels only as God wills. And God does not will that everyone observe all the counsels (or *all* the heroic ways of being generous), but only those that are suitable according to the variety of persons and their circumstances and abilities, as charity demands." When opportunity is given and accompanying factors do not indicate otherwise, the counsels of poverty, chastity and obedience are recognized as something that in themselves are wiser for us to follow than not to follow, because of their excellence. But such Divine counsels are not the Ten Commandments. They "are given for the perfection of Christians in general, not for the perfection of each one in particular." If one's father or mother "has true needs of one's assistance for their support, it is no time to practice the counsel of entering the monastery." Charity, which is "queen of all virtues, of all commandments, of all counsels, of all laws and Christian behavior, assigns to each of these its place, order, time and value..."

"Suppose you are a prince," continues the Saint, who must "beget heirs to secure your nation against tyranny, sedition and civil war. The circumstance of these benefits obliges you to beget lawful heirs in holy matrimony. This sacrificing virginal chastity for the public good is not to disown chastity, but rather to forgo it chastely in favor of charity... Charity not only does not permit fathers of families to sell all their property and proceeds to the poor, but it requires these men to acquire in an upright way what is needful to care for their household" (*Love of God*, Bk. 8, c. 6).

Another recommendation: The selection of a strictly contemplative community requires more care and special prudence. We are dealing with religious life at its height, which should be an *"antechamber to paradise,"* as St. Thérèse of Lisieux said of her Carmel community — a life lived at the summit of the Christian and religious virtues, a life of heavenly love which constitutes the heart of the whole Church. Here the gift of self is something radical, being of both soul and body. Here no pampering is granted to fallen nature, for all becomes something transcending fallen nature, through a constant, daily heroism. The preparation and the internal dispositions ought to be those of one who ventures forth into a martyrdom of love, a fire with slow-burning flame day and night.

Let the young reader pay serious attention. If the Lord is calling you, know how to choose the religious family generously and prudently which ought to help you to rise quickly in holiness. Do not be neglectful and unserious in the way you choose! Every consecrated life ought to be outstanding in love and heroic sacrifice.

THE MISSIONARY VOCATION

In the Acts of the Apostles we read that one night in a vision St. Paul saw a pagan of Macedonia calling him: *"Come, over and help us!"* (Acts 16: 19).

From mission lands, from pagan peoples, from non-believing nations, we Christians should constantly perceive the same cry addressed to us: *"Come... help us!"*

These people have a right to call upon us; for to us the command has been given by the Lord to go to them — *"Go you into the whole world and preach the Gospel to every creature" (Mk.* 16: 15). And the Church never grows weary of making her appeal for a generous response to God's summons to go "preach the Gospel and implant the Church among peoples and societies that do not yet believe in Christ" (Vatican II, *Ad Gentes*, n. 6).

Sad to say, this summons, though it is from the Lord Himself, often falls on deaf ears and goes unheeded. Once when St. Francis Xavier had preached to some Japanese people about God's immense love in sending us His only-begotten Son, someone made this complaint: "How is it that God, if He is as good as you say, has waited so many years to let us know the truths of Christianity?"

The Saint was deeply moved, and sighed. Then he answered, "Do you want to know? Here is the answer:

God had given many Christians the task of coming and preaching the Gospel to you; but many of these men did not wish to heed the summons".

That is precisely the way it is. We know very well that God *"wants everyone to be saved and reach full knowledge of the truth"* (I Tim. 2: 4). Therefore, He cannot have failed to call men to preach the Gospel of salvation to their fellow men who lacked the Faith. His calls surely have been often renewed; for, as St. John Chrysostom says, "God takes nothing so much to heart as the salvation of souls, and no work is more pleasing to Him".

Many had been called, but they "did not wish to heed the summons", St. Francis Xavier said sadly. This disobedience carries a heavy responsibility.

The missionary vocation is one of the noblest vocations in the Church. It is rightly compared with martyrdom and, in substance, it is a vocation to be a martyr. Consider, for example, the missionaries who were martyred in Morocco, in Japan, in the Philippines, in Turkey, in Uganda. If today it is not so easy to be a martyr, the missionary vocation still calls for aspiring and being ready to immolate oneself entirely. Thus the missionary can always repeat with St. Paul, *"I most gladly will spend and be spent myself for your souls"* (II Cor. 12: 15). He should be ready to die alone on an island, like St. Francis Xavier; to take his rest with a stone for a pillow, like St. Justin de Jacobis; to be strangled, like Blessed Francis Clet and Blessed Gabriel Perboyre; or to be crucified, as some Japanese martyrs were; or to be beheaded, as were certain witnesses for the Faith in the Philippines, and Blessed Theophane Venard in Indochina.

The missionary vocation is the vocation of brave souls, of generous, courageous hearts possessing a fearless and firm faith; for the Kingdom of Heaven "suffers violence and the violent bear it away" (Mt. 11: 12). It is a vocation for chosen persons, and in the strict sense not for all; although her missionary responsibilities, as Vat. II says, must concern the whole Church, which is the "light and salvation for the nations".

In every age after the Apostles, the Church has had great missionaries who have evangelized whole peoples and nations, such as St. Remigius, who brought Christ to France; St. Martin, who brought Him to Switzerland; St. Augustine of Canterbury, who evangelized England; St. Boniface, Germany; Sts. Cyril and Methodius, Bohemia and Illyria in Greece; St. Adalbert, Russia and Poland; without mentioning great Saints among the laymen who greatly aided the spread of the Gospel, as St. Stephen in Hungary and St. Wenceslaus in Bohemia.

Then there have been the religious Orders and Congregations, including the Franciscans, with St. Francis having spent a short time in Syria, and St. Anthony of Padua, whom a shipwreck prevented from reaching Morocco. The religious orders have sent missionaries to all continents— to Africa, to Asia, to the Near East and the Far East. And they have left us heroic examples, like that of the recent Blessed Damian Veuster, apostle to the lepers on the island of Molokai; Cardinal Massaia; St. Justin de Jacobis; Father Daniel Comboni; and many others.

One has but to read the Church's annual reports on mission activity or the annals published by missionary congregations, in order to understand the missionary effort of the Church, with its often deeply moving experiences that sometimes show incredible heroism.

One instance comes to mind of an appeal that the Foundress of the Franciscan Missionary Sisters of Mary of the Passion, made to all her Sisters. She wanted to send a group of six sisters to work with lepers in Burma, and she asked for volunteers. Over a thousand sisters answered the appeal and wanted to set out! A thousand noble, generous hearts. It was a great consolation to the Foundress, who assembled together the thousand replies and often said, "This is my golden book!"

Here is a striking letter that was written by Blessed Theophane Venard, a missionary who died a martyr in the Far East at Amman. In it he tells his sister Melania some of his incredible experiences. He wrote it shortly before his martyrdom:

"My dear sister: This year we have had an extraordinary flood. The water in my house was a foot deep. I saw fish, toads, frogs, crabs, snakes playing about in my room while I sat on some planks a couple of inches above the water level.

"Sister, this will surely startle you, but you ought to know that it has been worse. Mice have gone to sleep on my bedside mat, and one night I unfortunately crushed one. The poor thing startled me, but it saved me from danger. For when I moved the bed covers I discovered a poisonous snake with black and white stripes which had noiselessly climbed up on my bed and was snuggled in a corner where my feet extended."

This short letter gives us a vivid account of the perils, the adventures, the fears and the graces of the missionary. One cannot help being moved at the sight of these brave lovers of Christ who play with death and the glory of martyrdom in order to save the souls of their fellow men. What a grand credit they are to the missionary vocation!

However, today the Church is faced with a sad fact— more so than yesterday. It is this: missionaries are few, too few, and their number is diminishing instead of growing. During the Holy Year 1975, Pope Paul VI lamented the "sad phenomenon which has been noticeable to all for some time. We mean the decrease in the number of missionary vocations, precisely now at the very time when it is so necessary to direct more manpower to our missions ..."

Pius XI's words addressed to directors of various pontifical missionary projects, seem even more timely and significant today. The Pope said, "A man of high rank who, during the last war was not the highest in command but had a certain responsibility, with many men under his authority, saw fit to tell me, 'You cannot imagine the pain, the distress, the near despair one feels when his duty is to have the command of certain men and to lead them ahead, while he knows that they cannot advance because they lack ammunition, they lack equipment, because the nation is not producing enough for them...'

"This remark, spoken in the midst of the grim realities of blood and death, left me with a very pained impression, which is renewed every time I recall that conversation. Now we need to draw a lesson out of this.

What can be more painful, more tragic, for the missionary, than to have to bring a halt to his work or withdraw from it because he lacks the means to carry it on?..."

People need to be shaken. If they are Christian, they ought to become aware of the serious missionary problem. There are countless men waiting to receive the Gospel and to be fed the bread of truth and eternal life, *"children asking for bread, and never a crust to share with them!"* (Lam. 4: 4).

It is necessary to pray a great deal about this. *"The harvest indeed is great, but the laborers are few. Pray you therefore the Lord of the harvest that He send laborers into His harvest"* (Lk. 10:2). It is urgent that we appeal to the Lord that He deign to grant many missionaries to His Church.

If, then, anyone is called by God to the missionary life, let him not play deaf; let him not shirk the call; let him not refuse a vocation that is so sublime, a vocation drawing all its energies and lifeblood from Divine Love. And let it not be said that we should prefer to do missionary work in our own country. Instead, consider that not even five percent of the Church's missionary potential is functioning to bring the Gospel to the thousands of millions of non-Christians. Thus, how unseemly it would be to take even one vocation away from the small group of missionaries devoted to saving four-fifths of mankind, while just a fifth are served by almost half a million priests!

In his appeal to university students, St. Francis Xavier wisely said, "How I would like to go to the universities of Paris and the Sorbonne and address many men who are richer in learning than in zeal, to let them know the great number of souls who, because of their neglect, are deprived of grace and are apt to go to hell. There are millions of nonbelievers who would become Christian if there were missionaries."

Call to mind Jesus' words, *"Other sheep I have that are not of this fold: Them also I must bring... and they shall be one fold and one shepherd"* (Jn. 10: 16). As one reflects on these words, he sees the meaning of all the heroic accomplishments of our missionaries and the burning zeal of the two heavenly Patrons of the missions: "Just let me sail over treacherous seas and save a single soul, and then I would die content" (St. Francis Xavier). "Oh, how I would like to have been a missionary from the time of creation and continue to be one until the end of the world!" (St. Thérèse of Lisieux).

We ask young readers to listen and ponder. Do you not appreciate how great is a life consecrated to saving our non-believing brothers? If you were in their place, how you would long to meet a missionary who would bring you the saving truths of the Gospel! And perhaps Our Lord is calling you, and you perhaps are not heeding the call, but prefer to be a Christian who "stands idle" (Mt. 10: 6) *and does not labor in the Lord's vineyard.*

Be not like men who "do not consider within the heart" (Jer. 12: 11). *Give attention to these meaningful words of Our Lord, which might serve as instruments of grace for you and many young people like you* "Behold,... lift up your eyes, and see the countries. For they are white, all ready to harvest." (Jn. 4: 35)

OUR LADY AND VOCATIONS

When St. Maximilian Maria Kolbe was a boy of six he was high-spirited. He was a very good, industrious boy, but was playful and boiling over with energy. One day he played an unfortunate prank, and his good mother said, "Son, what will become of you?"

This question grieved him so that from that time on he became sad and silent. He thought it over, wept over it, and prayed about it. At the foot of the altar the little boy asked Our Lady for the answer to his mother's distressing question.

Our Lady chose to answer in person these innocent prayers. She appeared to little Raymond (Maximilian's name when he lived at home). She showed him two crowns in Her hands— one white and one red, and gave him to understand the white crown meant the consecrated, virginal life, while the red crown meant martyrdom. Our Lady asked the child which of the two crowns he wanted. He stretched out his little hands to take them both. Our Lady smiled and vanished. These were the Marian roots of St. Maximilian's vocation— this charming knight of the Immaculate, Her devoted apostle, who was capable of *"Marianizing"* everything that he planned and carried out, who ventured to avail himself of every legitimate means, great or small, in order to bring the Immaculate everywhere as the dawn of salvation for every soul, as one who would beget Jesus in every heart that beats on earth.

From his own wonderful experience, St. Maximilian can declare with firm assurance that Our Lady is the Mother of vocations, that She is a Mother to consecrated souls, a Mother of priests, and the heavenly educator of Saints.

We do not know directly about the birth of every vocation, but we know that the Mother of grace truly proves Herself the Mother and channel of this choice grace, and that no calling to a Divine vocation can come about without Our Lady having a direct hand in it.

If we could discover the personal secrets about the vocation of every Saint, in every one of them we would see Mary's motherly attentions carried out with every care.

For example, we know that St. Francis of Assisi discovered his true vocation in the little church of St. Mary of the Angels. From that little Marian church, as from the Immaculate Heart, the Franciscan Order emerged and spread throughout the world, and in that Marian nursery St. Francis wanted to end his seraphic mission on earth.

Many times Our Lady has awakened a vocation and then accompanied it on its way and saved it from sure ruin. There is the case of St. Gabriel of the Sorrowful Mother. This high-spirited young man was taking a chance of losing the gift he had from God of a vocation. During a procession at Spoleto in which an image of the

Blessed Virgin was being carried, the youth perceived that Mary's motherly eyes were fixed on him and within his heart he heard Her say, *"Francis, Francis, the world is not for you. Yours is the religious life."*

This maternal summons shocked Francis Possenti, enlightened him about the dangerous way he was taking in the world, and spurred him to reach the firm decision to enter the Passionists. He entered, and in a few years became a Saint.

And how can we forget the case of the holy Curé of Ars, St. John Vianney? No matter how hard he studied, John's lessons seemed insufficiently prepared to certain professors. When he appeared for the examinations for ordination, he did not satisfy the examiners in theology, who judged him unsuited for the priesthood. But the Father Rector knew something very important about this candidate. He knew that he greatly loved Our Lady and said the Rosary a great deal. So John's case was re-studied, and he was ordained. Indeed he had found studies difficult, being older than the other students; but by Our Lady's help and his own hard work at his books, the Saint had, more than others realized, *"rendered himself competent to discharge his great ministry."* His natural aptitude *"was not as meager as popular opinion would have it."* In the final judgment he enjoyed a *"clear mind and a right discernment"* (Pope John XXIII, *Encyclical Sacerdoti nostri,* III.)

St. Stanislaus Kostka had no less trouble in saving his religious vocation. Our Lady appeared to him once to direct him to not wait any longer but to set out from Vienna to Rome in order to enter the Society of Jesus.

Along the way She protected him from his brother, who was pursuing him in order to stop him at all costs from entering the Jesuits. Out of his childlike gratitude, St. Stanislaus was very devoted to Our Lady throughout his years as a religious. And Our Lady, in Her turn, enabled him to become a Saint, and in a short time called him to paradise on a Marian feast day, namely, the Assumption.

Another example where Our Lady saved a vocation is found in the life of St. Peter Chanel, martyr of Oceana. Peter put great effort in his studies in the seminary, but was not succeeding. Failures to satisfy the professors were discouraging him and he considered dropping his studies and returning home. At that juncture he happened to confide his problem to a pious person, who remarked, "Before quitting, have you consulted Our Lady?"

"No," Peter answered.

"Then first go to the Church and pray to Our Lady."

Peter followed the counsel, went to the Church, and prayed a long time at the foot of an image of Our Lady. Then he returned to his pious counselor. Full of peace and zeal to go ahead, he said, *"I prayed to our Lady, and I'll stay!"* Our Lady had saved his vocation to be a priest and a martyr. Such was his gratitude that once he pricked himself to get a drop of his blood, dipped his pen in it, and wrote, "Love Our Lady and make Her loved!"

Sometimes the grace of vocation comes together with the grace of conversion from a disordered life. Our Lady then both converts and calls to God's service at the same time. This is what happened to St. Camillus de' Lellis. He had led an unstable life, without ever setting down to anything. One day, returning from San Giovanni Rotondo to Manfredonia, halfway down the Gargano, he suddenly confronted a brilliant light, which also enlightened his mind about his pitiable, sinful state, and aroused him so strongly to repentance that he paused a long time to weep bitter tears. From that time on he was determined to radically change his life and give himself completely to God. He began to wonder how he happened to receive such an extraordinary grace on that particular day, and then he remembered it was February 2, the Feast of Our Lady's Purification. Then he exclaimed, *"Now I know who won this great grace for me!"*

Our Lady watches over all Her children, but in a special way over those whom Jesus has chosen to be "His own." If those who are called are favored by Jesus, they cannot fail to be likewise favored by Mary. And who can ever describe Our Lady's tender motherly attention to those whom God has "chosen", those who are to be the "ministers" of the Lord, or to be "spouses" of Christ?

We have two angelic examples — St. Bernadette and St. Thérèse of Lisieux, whom Our Lady herself shaped and polished to become gems of priceless beauty.

Was not the vocation of St. Bernadette clearly marked out and hallowed by the Immaculate Mother's presence? Why did Bernadette feel the urge to sacrifice herself in the religious life? Simply because *"when one sees Our Lady one wants nothing more of this world."*

The vision of Our Lady is enough to enkindle in a heart the urge to consecrate oneself to God. This is what happened with little Melanie, a seer of La Sallete. It happened likewise with Sister Lucy, the seer of Fatima.

The same happened with St. Thérèse of Lisieux, when she saw Our Lady's heavenly smile, which cured her of a severe sickness. From that "smile", St. Thérèse gained a renewed assurance that the Mother of God was watching over Her "little flower" with attention and was taking care "to make it grow straight and strengthen it in such a way that, five years later, it could open its petals on the fertile mountain of Carmel."

At this point we can also say that Our Lady not only watches over every vocation, but She has been the heavenly inspiration of Orders and Institutes that take just pride in being "Marian." We owe thanks to the Immaculate Mother for all consecrated souls, for She who is *"full of grace"* (Lk. 1: 28) has been the channel of Divine aid for us all, as St. Bernard says, and She ranks first among the elect, first among the consecrated souls, first among Jesus' followers, first among true religious, first among ministers of the Redemption, first among virgins and parents as Virgin Mother of God and of mankind.

Let the young reader give attention and reflection to what we say. If you want a vocation to the consecrated life because you do not have one, turn to Our Lady. Of course we should never pray, "Lord, if the favor I ask does not suit your plans, please change them" but a person's desire for this noble favor and appreciation of its value may be a grace indicating that God wants to hear him and grant him the vocation, as something intended for him from all eternity to acquire in this way.

If you already have this vocation and simply want to perfectly preserve it and fulfill it, then entrust it to Our Lady. If you are in danger of losing it, appeal at once to Her. She will even work miracles to preserve this "gift" of God for you, provided you hasten to Her with childlike trust and affection. You may then hope that She will enable you to reach paradise by way of Her own path, namely, consecration to God.

Young St. Thomas Aquinas, girded with the sash of purity by the angels after driving away the prostitute with a flaming torch.

COMMON QUESTIONS:

To whom should we disclose our first serious thoughts of becoming a "follower of Jesus" as a priest, a religious brother or sister?

As a rule, one ought to disclose it to one's Confessor or Spiritual Director, not to one's parents or kindred, unless one is quite sure that they are well disposed toward the priestly and religious calling.

If the confessor at once shows opposition to our considering such a vocation, is it lawful to seek counsel of another priest?

It is lawful, but one should be prudent about whom he consults and what he says, explaining the likely reasons for the other priest's opposition. In particular cases one obviously can even change confessors, going to one who is willing to examine our case and help us decide about our vocation.

At what age should one follow through on God's call?

The ideal time is anywhere from the fifteenth to the twenty-fifth year of age. Before fifteen things are very uncertain about the future. After thirty it is harder to change one's ways and submit to a program of formation.

Then must one who is thirty or older give up the idea of entering the consecrated life?

He need not to "give it up". There have been and always will be exceptions to the rule, and not a few persons in their thirties have consecrated themselves to God and become great Saints. But from thirty years on it is always harder to fit into a different system of life and adjust to a different outlook. The best illustration is that of a plant which has been growing in a given direction. As long as it is only a shrub one can bend it and straighten it to take the direction one wants. But once it is a tree, it more easily breaks than bends. Thus one who enters religion at such an age must be ready to do great violence to himself in accepting formation if he wants to sanctify himself.

If in senior high school or as a college freshman one begins to discover his vocation to a consecrated life, what should be done?

One needs the guidance of a spiritual director to decide on the best time to follow God's call to leave all to follow Christ. As a rule, in senior high school one could wait till he finished his final examinations. This waiting period, used well, can serve to give depth and firmness to his vocation, at the same time enabling him to finish the studies he had begun.

If one is a college freshman, several things need to be considered. Perhaps the vocation needs a ripening period, to be provided in the remaining years of college, if there are good safeguards there for his spiritual life. Then you have to consider the type of consecrated life chosen, which might or might not profit by attendance at college. One will need to consult to see whether it is better to quit college at once.

What are the moral qualifications necessary for entering the consecrated life?

a) *A right intention.* One should not go to a seminary or religious community out of fear of the temporal hardships of living in the world, nor for fear of offending someone, nor to satisfy temporal interests or escape being jobless, nor from false ideas about the life, and certainly not for the thrill of adventure.

b) *Upright morals.* It is good if one comes with unsullied innocence. But there are souls which, after their conversion, have beautifully persevered and become Saints. It is enough that one have reached such a stable condition of faith and supernatural virtue, as to give assurance that he will persevere and grow in them.

c) *A delicate conscience.* A conscience that not only avoids super-scrupulosity and laxity, but shows itself well-balanced, prudent, and conscientious about one's responsibilities.

d) *A fair amount of intelligence — at least.* One need not be a genius, but he must be able to grasp the essentials about what consecration to God means and its value, he must appreciate his duty to fulfill this consecration and be able intelligently to carry out his assigned tasks.

For the priesthood obviously one must have the ability to complete studies of philosophy and theology.

What conditions are required as to health for entering a seminary or religious house?

Ordinary good health is necessary. The burdens of priestly and religious life are certainly not light ones. Good health is needed in order to be faithful to duty and carry out one's mission; but, of course, it need not be the robustness of Samson.

Are there some diseases that hinder one from becoming a priest or religious brother or sister?

Yes. Examples are:

Mental ailments. — Obviously by nature these are grave and they may be incurable. A good mental-physical balance is of primary importance for a life consecrated to the service of God and one's fellow man in a religious community.

There are other diseases, too, like blindness, paralysis, epilepsy, syphilis, and any other incurable illness affecting one's vital organs.

Is the inversion of the sexual tendency of a man or woman a grave moral obstacle to the priestly or religious life? Or perhaps could it be one of the best suited ways to heal this anomaly?

The Church has always considered homosexuality and lesbianism to be grave obstacles. The reasons are easily appreciated. It suffices to consider the danger of likely irreparable scandal.

A great physician and psychologist declared that the foolish thought that one might heal a homosexual youth by putting him in a male institution is the same as trying to cure another man of the habit of seducing women by putting him in a women's institution.

To whom should one apply for directions for entering a seminary?

Ordinarily to one's pastor, who can give all the necessary practical directions. Also, one may apply directly to the Seminary Rector.

What school certificates are needed, and how many years of school are necessary for the priesthood?

One must present a high school diploma in order to enter the courses of philosophy and theology that are required for the priesthood.

The courses of philosophy and theology required for ordination last six years ordinarily.

To whom does one apply who would enter a religious community and what papers should he present?

He should first of all ask the priest who gives him spiritual guidance. That priest can arrange for him to interview the proper person, or he can give him or her directions about how to obtain such an interview.

The documents ordinarily required are a birth certificate, baptismal and confirmation certificates, certificates of residence (for Italy), of freedom from impediments, and of health (from a physician), a letter of recommendation from one's pastor or spiritual father, school transcripts, military discharge papers (if one has been in the service).

Are there different decrees of approval on the part of the Church of religious institutes?

Yes. Some religious institutes are approved only by the Bishop of the diocese, and some are approved by the Holy See. The first kind are called institutes of diocesan right, and the second are institutes of pontifical right. Every religious institute which develops and flourishes becomes rather easily one of pontifical right.

What are the vows of religious and when are they taken?

The vows are three: obedience, poverty, and chastity.

The vows are ordinarily taken at two times: namely, at the end of the year of novitiate (this is called *temporary profession*), and at the end of period of temporary vows, which are for a minimum of three years and a maximum of nine years. The final vows are called *perpetual profession.*

Are any school transcripts needed for entering religious as a religious lay brother?

Transcripts showing completion of the first eight grades are as a rule needed. But this might not always be possible by reason of age or some other cause. In that case proof of sufficient maturity is required.

May one who is an only child abandon his or her parents to enter a seminary or religious community?

One assuredly can, provided the parents both agree. It is a serious matter, and the Church requires the parents' consent. Otherwise she considers it her duty not to accept the candidate. But there are some few courageous parents who know how to offer their only son or daughter to God!

How can one make sure that he is called by God?

One needs to follow the course established by the Church; that is, let oneself be guided and be assured by a spiritual Father once your case has been well weighed. As a rule no one is better than he in this field. It will not help you to go about consulting here and there this one and that one. Nearly always one wastes time that way and becomes confused.

Much less should you look for miraculous signs or extraordinary revelations. A great deal of prayer, a certain time spent in reflection, and the guidance of your spiritual Father are the best ways of making sure of a call from God.

What if the parents are decisively against the vocation and want to hinder at all costs their son or daughter from entering the religious life?

Here it is enough that we recall the example of St. Francis and St. Clare of Assisi, who had to run away from home in order to dedicate themselves to God. Likewise St. Thomas Aquinas and St. Teresa of Avila fled from their homes.

When the parents' opposition is unreasonable, one should, with reverence and respect, if truly called by God to the consecrated life, recall the words of St. Peter and St. John to the chief priests who opposed them: "*If it be just in the sight of God, to hear you rather than God, decide for yourselves*" (Acts 4: 19); and Our Lord's own words:

"He who loves father or mother more than Me is not worthy of Me" (Mt. 10: 37)

What thought or sentiment should one keep uppermost who wants to "follow Jesus"? Can you present something to keep in mind?

The thought that appeals to me is this sublime reflection of St. Paul: *"But the things that were gain to me, the same I have counted loss for Christ. Furthermore, I count all things to be but loss for the excellent knowledge of Jesus Christ, my Lord: for whom I have suffered the loss of all things and count them but as dung, that I may gain Christ."* (Phil. 3: 7-8)

Eucharistic-Marian Reading

Obviously there is a need for good, solid devotional books on Marian Shrines and Saints... The Franciscan Friars of the Immaculate are attempting to meet this need at a reasonable cost.

A Handbook on Guadalupe
The latest, authoritative book on Guadalupe covers the theme with 40 topical chapters, written by leading experts on Guadalupe. A treasure of facts and insights, with many new exciting discoveries.

St. Thérèse: Doctor of the Little Way
Among the many books about St. Thèrèse, this one is unique because it offers a compendium of insights from 23 writers who have contributed chapters on all aspects of the life and spirituality of this new Doctor of the Church.

Jesus Our Eucharistic Love *by Fr. Stefano Manelli, F.I.*
This little treasure of Eucharistic devotion is based on the writing and examples taken from the lives of the Saints.

All Generations Shall Call Me Blessed *by Fr. Manelli, F.I.*
This clear and concise exposition of Mary as Virgin-Mother and Queen (all Biblical) is an ideal way of explaining her vital role in the economy of Salvation.